CORE LIVING
8 Choices for Living Well

Harry Stefanakis Ph.D.

Copyright © 2017 Harry Stefanakis

All rights reserved.

ISBN: 1975654560
ISBN-13: 987-1975654566

DEDICATION

This book is dedicated to my clients for demonstrating the courage to change and for honoring me with the privilege of taking a part of their journey with them.

CONTENTS

	Acknowledgments	i
	Introduction	1
1	Steering the mind	5
2	You are what you consume	18
3	How to get out of a 10 foot hole	28
4	Like riding a bike	38
5	Lemonade, fertilizer and the art of reframing	51
6	Tricksters, boxes and possibilities	61
7	Living the dash	74
8	The connection imperative	87
	Eight Choices: Summary	101
9	CORE Practices	104
	Source Notes	140

ACKNOWLEDGMENTS

There is an old expression that indicates that if we see or discover truth, it is only by virtue of sitting on the shoulders of giants. In my case these giants not only refer to the scientists, philosophers and teachers that have taught me in one way or another, but also my clients who teach me daily about life transformation and inspire me with their courage. I dedicate this book to them. There are still other giants who have supported me in completing this book. My wife's persistent encouragement and belief, including the push to get this done before our son arrives, was invaluable to me. Thank you Rochelle. My colleagues who have supported me and my work throughout the years. There are too many to mention them all here but a special thanks to Dale for the years of comradery as we evolved our practices next to each other. I must also mention my friend Darcy for setting up an accountability process to keep me on track. It worked! There were also the friends that encouraged, read, edited and/or provided gentle feedback. Many thanks to Daryl, Don, Hari, Liz, Peter and Stephane.

INTRODUCTION

Be the change you want to see in the world.
                                         Gandhi

I wrote this book, at the encouragement of many of my clients, to express some straight forward ideas that I have identified and developed over the course of my career. These ideas, and the practices that accompany them, can have a profound impact on our lives, if we choose to apply them. Books that offer useful information in a clear and accessible way inspired me and I wanted to write something similarly practical and concise.

Throughout the book, I endeavor to capture your attention in heart and mind. I present you with stories[1] that reflect simple truths and I have backed up these truths with scientific evidence. There is more scientific support for these ideas than I have cited. Other authors have written wonderful books with science leading and with stories playing a supporting role[2]. In this book, I wanted a different balance. I wanted you to relate to the material in a direct way even as I satisfied your logical mind with supporting evidence.

Each of the first eight chapters identifies a choice we can make that will move our lives towards well-being and success. Considering the information presented as choices is important because it highlights

---

[1] With respect to stories about my clients, I have changed the names and other information to protect the identities of these individuals.

[2] I have referenced a number of these books in the source notes.

our agency in life. It is true that we don't always choose in circumstances of our own making. Sometimes we find ourselves in unfortunate situations that are beyond our control. Nevertheless, we can still choose how to face the circumstances of our lives. By choosing we accept responsibility for our lives and in doing so we find our freedom.

As you read the book you will come across overlapping ideas. In essence, the book speaks to two key themes. The first theme is on the importance of cultivating attention properly. Attention is important because our brain creates neural networks from the experiences we focus on. In neuroscience, this is called experience dependent neuroplasticity. I begin the book explicitly with this theme on attention but you will notice that it arises again and again across various chapters. Throughout the book then, we explore why attention is critical, how we focus our attention, what pulls our attention, how it gets stuck, how to re-orient our attention and what can guide our attention.

Cultivating attention is a way of cultivating the right attitude towards life. As astronaut Chris Hatfield said in his book *An Astronaut's Guide to Life on Earth*, in space flight, attitude refers to one's orientation and maintaining your attitude could be the difference between life and death. He noted that therefore attitude is more important than any goals that are set out. He suggested that life on Earth is similar. "There's really just one thing I can control: my attitude towards the journey, which is what keeps me feeling steady and stable, and what keeps me headed in the right direction. So, I consciously monitor and correct, if necessary, because losing attitude would be far worse than not achieving my goal."

The second theme is also seen throughout the book but is made explicit in chapter eight. This theme involves understanding the importance of intelligent compassion as the bridge between two complimentary truths of human existence. One truth, based on the reality of our independent physical bodies, reflects our experience of separation from each other and the consequent need for survival. The other truth refers to the reality of an underlying unity and is associated with our need for connection and growth. [3]

You will note that I speak of intelligent compassion because all too often we get lost in a narrow understanding of compassion as a soft emotion. This narrow view creates both compassion fatigue (where we burn out in caring) and compassion anxiety (where we avoid compassion out of fear that others will take advantage of us). Consequently, I invite you to consider compassion from a broader perspective. Through the lens of intelligent compassion, you will find a more complete and scientifically valid perspective that includes compassion for self and others equally. Intelligent compassion also broadens our understanding of how to respond to life by promoting skillful engagement in the world. In this way, we create more effective and functional relationships with ourselves and others that facilitates movement towards health, success and well-being for all.

---

[3] Physicist David Bohm called this underlying unity "the implicate order." to describe the deeper (quantum) reality in which energy, matter and information (life), are entangled or interconnected and out of which the physical reality we see unfolds (Bohm referred to the physical reality as "the explicate order").

Regardless of how well a book is written or how informative it is, books don't change people. People change themselves by making choices and acting on those choices. Each of the first eight chapter, therefore, offers some ideas for applying what you have learned and I complete this book in the final chapter with a framework that describes a set of CORE principles and practices. The CORE practices represent four complementary sets of exercises that help connect us to our resourcefulness, build our capacity and instill resilience to live effectively in the world.

The practices are an invitation to apply the messages of the book so that knowledge is mobilized into life affirming change. Many of the practices are reflections or distillations from a variety of wisdom traditions and they are grounded in scientific evidence. Simply put they work. They do require effort and commitment though. These practices are not magical rituals that have immediate transformative powers. Instead, with practice and engagement you find yourself living more effectively and peacefully in the world.

I hope that as you read the book, you find it both inspirational and aspirational. That you discover truths about the human journey and find those truths grounded in evidence, so that both your heart and mind open to the possibilities of your life. By opening to possibilities and releasing restraints, may you be moved to act in ways that support your life and the world.

CHAPTER 1

STEERING THE MIND

"When we focus on something we amplify it in our awareness. Focus is not what helps or hurts - it's the quality and direction of the focus that makes a difference in what and how we feel." Michael Yapko

STEERING THE MIND

I remember the day my father removed the training wheels off the back wheel of my bronze banana seat bike. I was five years old and I felt both excited and nervous. I remember him holding the back of the bike as I started to peddle, how he ran along holding on for a few seconds, then he released and I was alone. It was exhilarating. At first all I saw was open space. A wide laneway offering freedom. Then I remember seeing this one rock in the middle of the laneway (in my mind it appeared incredibly large). I remember thinking "I'll be fine as long as I don't hit that rock." A thought I fixated on, "I'll be fine as long as I don't hit that rock," "I'll be fine as long as I don't hit that rock." This thought focused my eyes on the rock so that was all I saw. The rock that I so wanted to avoid became my whole world at that point. The exhilaration was gone and replaced by a fear of falling and being embarrassed. You can guess what happened next. Of course, I rode right to that rock and lost my balance. On the other hand, if I had continued to focus on the open road I would have been fine.

That was my first lesson in attention. I have learned since that cultivating attention is critical to living well. This chapter is about focus and attention. I use these terms synonymously because to attend to something properly our focus must be directed there. Attention is the steering wheel of our lives. Whatever we focus on will not only expand in our consciousness, we also tend to move towards the object of our attention whether that object is internal (e.g., pain or anxiety) or external (e.g., poverty, procrastination, indulgence or a rock). That early life event taught me an important lesson not only for cycling but for life. Now as I move forward in my life I keep my view open and I try to focus on where I want to go rather than the obstacles that I see along the way.

Attention is important because we receive millions of bits of information from our external and internal environments every second. Consciously we can only process about forty bits of this information at a time. What we select to focus on will therefore have real implications on our lives.

Our reality always includes our strengths, resources and blessings as well as our shortcomings, challenges and misfortunes. If we focus exclusively on our shortcomings or misfortunes we begin to see ourselves and our life in a narrow way and respond to our circumstances from this narrow view. Successful people, on the other hand, can see their shortcomings and misfortunes but they have also learned to focus on their strengths and resources. They have learned to acknowledge their blessings and to share them. How we cultivate our focus and attention is, therefore, critical to creating an exceptional life. What does it mean, however, to cultivate one's attention properly?

In my teaching and clinical work, I frequently use a driving metaphor to help people understand this idea. When we first learn to  drive, we are all supposed to also learn how to get out of skid in a car (for example, when you hit black ice or hydroplane on a slick road). That's because people make two consistent mistakes when they start skidding. First, they slam on the brakes which will lock the wheels and can spin the car further out of control (less of an issue now with ABS breaks). Second, they fixate on what they don't want to hit. When you fixate on what you don't want to hit (e.g., the tree that you are facing) you increase the probability of moving in that direction (or over correcting and hitting the tree on the other side).

The same is true in life. When people are in a skid in life, which can involve experiencing some difficulty or life challenge (e.g., illness, injury, employment or relationship issues, etc.) they may try and stop everything. Some of my clients, for example, start to avoid aspects of their lives (e.g., people, places, topics) and become afraid, passive and resentful. Others blame themselves for their difficulties, isolate themselves from their family and friends and feel more and more alone in their lives. Avoidance and isolation often spiral people towards clinical depression making the skid much worse. Just like with automobiles, slowing down (gearing down) when you are in a life skid is useful, trying to stop completely and suddenly is not.

Perhaps worse than trying to stop everything is fixating on what you don't want. One way to recognize this in yourself or someone else is the focus on "what if…catastrophe[4]" thinking. What if the pain doesn't go

---

[4] I call these quicksand questions because the more you ask them the more you get stuck. There are also positive what if questions that serve to open our minds to possibilities. These "beautiful" questions are explored in chapter nine.

away? What if I'm not accepted? What if I can't pay my bills? What if they don't like my book? What if...? What if...? What if...? When we focus on what we don't want, our mind and energy moves in that direction. We then begin to believe that the problem affects every aspect of our lives and that it will always do so.

The problem is that our mind does not work well with negation. If I ask you NOT to think about pink elephants right now what happens? When you try and not think about them you will notice that you immediately think about them. And the harder you try not to, the more difficult it becomes. A series of studies by Daniel Wegner and others demonstrated that when research participants were told not to think about something, a paradoxical effect was triggered whereby they would think more about that which they were trying to avoid. This effect is also evident when people try to avoid experiencing physical sensations or feelings. The more you try to avoid something the more it expands in your consciousness and can lead to engaging in the behaviours you wish to avoid. For example, if you try and supress thoughts about eating chocolate you are likely to eat more chocolate.

Recently I was teaching an introductory session on clinical hypnosis. Hypnosis is fundamentally about what we choose to focus on and what we choose to dissociate from. Remember by focusing on something we amplify it in our consciousness and in our experience. During a group experiential exercise one of the students suddenly began coughing. Her coughing became worse throughout the exercise and finally stopped once the exercise was over. I asked her after the exercise if she had any thoughts associated with her coughing. She acknowledged immediately that after she coughed she thought to herself "I hope I don't do this again." A thought that recurred after each time she coughed and soon included anxiety that she might cough again. The more she focused on not wanting to cough, the more she coughed. Essentially, she hypnotized herself into coughing again and again. In fact, not only does *what we think about expands in our consciousness, we are more likely to create what we are focusing* on even if what we are focusing on is what we are trying to avoid!

Learning to shift our focus can, therefore, be very useful. In the early years of my work at a physical rehabilitation center working with injured workers who were struggling with recovery and persistent pain, I would do this group exercise that I borrowed from psychologist Jon Kabat-Zinn. I would provide the participants in the rehabilitation program 3 raisins to eat. Sometimes I would have to give them extra because they would eat the raisins immediately and mindlessly before we could even start the exercise. Once everyone had the raisins, I would invite them to eat the raisins slowly, paying attention to the look and colour of the raisin, the texture of the raisin in their fingers, the sensation of their body as they slowly moved the raisin to their mouths, the emotions arising, the salivary response activating, the aroma as it approached the mouth, then the taste as they chewed slowly letting the flavours run across the whole tongue and finally noticing the swallow reflex kicking in and swallowing.

The whole process would take about 5 minutes. We

repeated it twice more. I would then ask the patients to discuss what they noticed. At first the conversation was about how good the raisins tasted (the raisins tasted good for most people, I discovered however, a minority who really don't like raisins). But then I asked them how much pain they remember experiencing during the three 5-minute exercises. The patients were shocked to note that, during the exercise, their pain was in the background of their awareness and not as bothersome or they didn't remember experiencing pain at all.

These were not magic raisins. Putting so much attention on one thing reduces energy in other areas. This is not only true for internal sensations but also for external perceptions. In one of the most famous experiments in psychology, Christopher Chabris and Daniel Simons showed that half the people in their studies would not see a dancing gorilla if their attention was focused on something else even when it passed into the middle of the object of their focus (check this and other videos for yourself at www.theinvisiblegorilla.com). Although this study shows how we can miss obvious things when we are distracted, it also points to how important it is to understand attention and how to cultivate it properly.

Let's return to our driving metaphor to explore how to apply this information. When in a skid in an automobile you increase the probability of getting out of the skid safely by looking in the direction that you want to go. The same is true in life. For example, another student in the hypnosis seminar was so focused on the exercise and her experience that she did not even notice the coughing (and it was loud) and instead reported a pleasant experience. The first choice for building a healthy and successful life therefore involves: choosing to focus on what we want to create in our life not what we wish to avoid. For example, we want to focus more on promoting health rather than avoiding pain, on eating well rather than avoiding certain foods, on creating wealth rather than avoiding poverty, on possibility instead of obstacles and as Mother Teresa pointed out we need to focus on creating peace rather than just being against war. So, ask yourself whether you are focusing on aspects of your life and experience that are helping you move forwards or whether your attention is locked on aspects of experience that keep you stuck and point you in the wrong direction?

To illustrate this further, let me tell you about Justin, a man I worked with in the British Columbia prison system. Justin had a horrible history both in terms of his own childhood experiences of neglect and victimization and then as an adult engaged in a lifestyle of violence and addiction. When I first met Justin, everyone called him sleeves because of his full arm tattoos. He appeared to carry that name as well as his violent history with pride. It wasn't too long, however, that I realized it wasn't pride he felt but resignation. He did not believe he could escape this life of violence any more than erase the tattoos that embellished his body. Every story he or others shared about his life included experiences of violence. He was even labeled by the system with the diagnosis of antisocial personality disorder. In essence, he was absorbed in aspects of his experience that worked against a healthy and productive life.

One day I asked him to tell me about some parts of his life that didn't involve violence, that in fact were the opposite of that life. I explained that no one's life is always just one way even if that is the majority of what they are doing and experiencing. What he told me was startling and a surprise to everyone in corrections. What he shared with me also set up a remarkable transformation in his life. He shared stories of rescuing animals that were being abused by others and nursing them back to health. He shared stories of looking for and finding useful items that others had thrown out, repairing them and giving them away as gifts. He shared stories of the birth of his daughter and his experience of peace when lost in a piece of art he was creating. In sharp contrast to the stories of pain, destruction and violence were these stories of healing, creation and peace.

Although we continued to maintain a focus on his responsibility for his violent actions we also began to focus on the Justin that healed, created and experienced peace. This became the new focus and direction for his life. The road was not perfect and he struggled with addiction until his life ended but he was never violent again. He reconnected with his family and his daughter. They shared with me how much he had changed and what a blessing it was to meet that part of him that moved towards peace and healing. I share this story in honour of the courage he showed to steer his life in a new direction by focusing on the kind of life he really wanted to create despite what others believed or said to him.

Shawn Achor, one of the worlds leading experts on happiness and success, has identified that a fulfilling life depends on one's realistic perception of the world. By realistic he is clear that he neither means optimistic or pessimistic but rather having a capacity to see broadly what is before you (both the good and the bad) and to believe in your capacity to face what is before you. In my work with Justin, we never ignored the truth of his experiences and use of violence. We simply added an equally true and infinitely more useful perspective that helped him move in a healthier direction.

Achor refers to this as a skill in creating a positive reality. It involves our capacity to see multiple truths at the same time (just as Justin learned to see the truth of his capacity for healing and creating in addition to truths about violence and destruction). This requires an ability to move our focus out in order to see broadly and then narrowly again once we have selected a more useful focus that is both true and positive.

My friend Daryl is an excellent example of someone who creates positive realities. Daryl was in an automobile accident when he was 19 years old and came out of that accident as a quadriplegic. Daryl shared with me that many people with spinal cord injuries get stuck in looking for the scientific miracle that will help them walk again. He indicated those that thrive after their accident tend to focus on creating their lives rather than waiting for a miracle. Daryl is one such individual. He didn't let his paralysis define him. He has created a successful and fulfilling life both professionally and by building a community of strong relationships. More than thirty years after his accident he still uses a manual chair and exercises regularly to maintain the best function he can. He travels extensively, he scuba dives and he volunteers his time to help others. He does have health challenges and systemic challenges (the world needs to do a much better job at supporting accessibility for all people) but he maintains a focus on the aspects of reality that work at supporting his life. Many people with injuries focus on what they lost, Daryl opened his gaze to what was possible given his reality and has built a wonderful and fulfilling life.

How can you learn to broaden your focus? One of the most critical skill that will be described in more detail in chapter nine involves learning to be centered and present. Mindfulness practices train us to stay nonjudgmentally present amid our experiences thereby shifting us from a narrow-fixed state to an open state.

For example, let me tell you about Ivan who developed an adjustment disorder with mixed anxiety and depression after retirement from his profession. In

---

TRY THIS: Basic Instructions for Practicing Mindfulness

1. Set Intention (e.g., I am now practicing mindfulness; I choose to be present; I am discovering what it is like to be present)
2. Set your Focus (e.g., on breath, on body, on mantra or scared words)
3. Set Attitude: strong and open posture; allow self to rest in noticing what is happening
4. Practice for 5 minutes. Notice and Acknowledge movement from focus to thoughts, memories, etc. and gently return to focus without judgement
5. Finish and reflect on the experience

Remember there is no way to fail. No right outcome.

our sessions, it became clear that Ivan's focus was on the past and what he was losing by retiring. He had difficulty focusing on anything else. He developed difficulties with short term memory, making decisions and focusing on anything (e.g., reading a book) for any length of time. I had discussed mindfulness practices with Ivan and because of his strong Christian faith I suggested the centering prayer where the focus, as described by Fr. Thomas Keating, involves choosing a scared word consistent with the faith. After a couple of weeks of practicing in this way, Ivan could let go of focusing on his past and he became more open to the possibilities that were available to him now that he was retired. His symptoms disappeared and he found renewed energy to focus on what he wanted to create in this next stage of his life. He was now facing his future instead of his past.

We can also train our capacity for seeing different perspective by practicing perspective taking directly. This training can be as simple as taking a new route to work or talking to a person or persons with whom you do not normally talk. These small changes take us out of our habits where we are on autopilot and allow for something new to enter our consciousness. These small changes can sometimes be enough to open our minds to new possibilities.

> **TRY THIS: Perspective Taking**
>
> - Take a new route to work
> - Talk to someone new
> - Use nondominant hand to open doors for two weeks
> - Look at an object you see everyday and identify as many aspects about it as you can

I frequently suggest to my clients a formal practice where they go and really notice trees. Typically, we see a tree and label it a tree and then move on thinking we understand what we have seen. But what happens if you slow down that process and really look at the next tree you come across. Walk around it. Notice the different colors and architecture from the different vantage points. Notice the sounds and how it can be teaming with a variety of different life forms. Feel the varieties of texture and notice the different aromas. Practices such as this train your perspective "muscle" increasing your capacity to see more without getting lost in what you see.

I invite you to notice what direction you are facing right now because your life is moving in that direction. **Choose to see more broadly and then focus on where you want to go instead of what you are trying to avoid.** This is essential for creating a realistic and positive attitude towards life. Don't forget that you can adjust your focus even if you are facing in the wrong direction. Identify what direction would serve you and turn in that direction.

Tree Man © Wendy McKinlay

Photographer Wendy McKinlay shared this photo with me of a tree on a busy downtown street in Vancouver. People just walked by it, but she noticed how some of the branches had shaped into a form that looked like man sitting on the tree.

CHAPTER 2

YOU ARE WHAT YOU CONSUME

"What our consciousness consumes becomes the substance of our life. So, we have to be very careful with which nutrients we ingest." Thich Nhat Hanh

YOU ARE WHAT YOU CONSUME

What would happen if you did not watch, listen to or read the news (including social media) for two weeks? This was the prescription I gave to two clients I was seeing in my private practice. They both came in to see me due to physical and psychological trauma after being in car accidents. Both had been rear-ended and suffered whip-lash injuries that included pain, severe anxiety and nightmares. After three months of treatment they were both better. They were driving again without anxiety, they were back at work and although they continued to experience some pain, it was under control. Additionally, the nightmares had stopped and they were sleeping well again. Just as I was preparing to end treatment, they both came into my office with all their symptoms back. Their nightmares had returned, their pain was elevated and their driving anxiety was back.

These two individuals did not know each other and neither had been in or witnessed any further accidents. What they did share was an experience we all shared. Their symptoms returned after the wars in Iraq and Afghanistan began. In my discussions with them I realized that they were glued to the news all day. They listened or watched in the morning when they were getting ready for work. They listened to the news on the radio while driving to work and they listened, read the paper and/or watched the news at work and at home after work. Conversations about these events also consumed most of their interactions. I recommended a simple remedy. No news for two weeks. After following this recommendation all their symptoms significantly reduced again. Their overconsumption of distressing news had, once again, shifted their whole experience of life to one that was unsafe. This had real effects on them both physically and psychologically. By stopping their negative consumption and refocusing on the tools they had learned through their course of therapy, they returned to health.

Research shows that both repetitions of words and visual cues in our environment can have an impact on our behaviour, even if we are unaware of it. For example, In one study researchers found that university students exposed to words they associated with the elderly (e.g., gray, wrinkled, bald), walked more slowly after exposure to these words compared to a group who was exposed to a different set of words. In another study researchers noted that people contributed three times more in the "honesty box" for coffee or tea in a common room when a picture of eyes was placed above the honesty box.

Similarly, our mood can be impacted through repetition of words or thoughts. In the late 1960s, cognitive psychologist Emmett Velten demonstrated that he could change the mood states of individuals by having them read different statement. He reported that when individuals read positive statements for 5 minutes their moods would shift to a positive state. If they read negative statements their moods would shift to negative states. The effect is even more pronounced when done with groups of people at the same time. Velten's mood induction technique is still used today and follow up research has confirmed that there is an impact from repeatedly hearing, saying or thinking specific kinds of statements.

Importantly, most of the time we are not even aware of all the images, thoughts and words that we are taking in because we receive millions of bits of information every day. Additionally, we often have a sense that any images, thoughts or words that repeat must be true or important otherwise they wouldn't repeat. It is no surprise then that in military training and emergency settings personnel are taught to repeat important information at least three times. My wife, a nurse educator, shared with me that in hospital settings, messages that were not repeated were simply considered as announcements that could be ignored, but if something was repeated you paid attention.

Moreover, words and images create associations in our minds that bring up similar information. Negative words, thoughts or images bring to mind other negative experiences of a similar nature multiplying the effect. Justin, for example, struggled with the messages about violence he heard about himself for much of his life. This information led him to the same bad choices in his life. That is until he could see that he didn't have to consume those messages. This brings me to another useful metaphor: *you become what you consume*, not just in terms of nutrition but also in terms of thoughts and information.

In behavioural research, this kind of influence is referred to as the priming effect. The words or images presented prime us to think and feel a certain way by capturing our attention, especially when consumed repeatedly. Studies have demonstrated that priming can influence how we judge others, whether we indulge in habits or avoid indulgence, how we perform on tests and can even increase or decrease prosocial responses in certain situations. Priming is more complicated in real life than it is in research studies but nevertheless it remains true that what we pay attention to, even unconsciously, can affect our mood and behaviour in profound ways. Advertisers are very familiar with this effect and use it constantly to attempt to influence our mood and decisions regarding the products and services they are promoting.

What makes priming more challenging is that we have a negativity bias. Basically, our brain is geared to look for negative information to protect us from danger. This negativity bias helped our ancestors survive immediate dangers, but it lowers our quality of life by effecting our mood and our ability to make good decisions in the complex modern world. Research in neuroscience and positive psychology has demonstrated that we can compensate for the negativity bias by increasing consumption of healthy information and reducing consumption of negative information.

Indeed, I often prescribe two-week news fasts, social media fasts and other forms of unplugging to my clients. Although we need to be aware of what is happening in the world and in our communities, all too often the news involves a repetition of mostly the negative events that have occurred and these are often presented in a sensational manner that activates fear and anxiety (e.g., "if it bleeds, it leads" is a common saying in newsrooms). Similarly, research on the impact on social media is demonstrating that overconsumption of Facebook or Twitter, for example, triggers anxiety as well as jealousy and other negative emotions. On the other hand, unplugging from technology and connecting with nature for four days can boost your creativity by 50%.

Sustained and heightened anxiety makes us dumb by constricting metabolic activity in our prefrontal cortex, the control center and executive functioning area of the brain. As health psychologist Kelly McGonigal points out, when we are in constant states of anxiety we are significantly more likely to give in to temptations, react instead of responding to life circumstances and we are less likely to remember our long-term goals or to stick with tasks that support our long-term health and success.

I was challenged once when presenting the idea of taking news or social media fasts by someone who indicated that I was asking people to "stick their heads in the sand" and not pay attention to what was going on. I am not advocating for that at all. The truth is that there is very little risk in taking news or information fasts. If something important is happening someone (who has not unplugged) will let us know and we can then have our fill of the information.

> **TRY THIS: Take Time to Unplug**
>
> - News and/or social media fast for two weeks (or longer)
> - Limit emailing to work hours
> - Consider one day a week where you will call or speak to someone face to face instead of texting
> - Establish a no media and no device zone (e.g., at dinner time or in the bedroom)
> - Spend time in nature without your devices

Additionally, I decided to do an informal experiment after this challenge. Another world crisis had occurred, the London subway bombings. In the days that followed the initial story, I challenged the group I was working with to pay attention and notice if there was any new information in the media or anything useful that they could apply in their lives regarding the crisis issue. It turns out the news reports that followed were mostly presenting "what if..." scenarios. "What if this happened in our subway?" "Is our port safe?" Indeed, I have noticed that frequently the news of an event is followed by speculation of a similar event occurring again or closer to one's home regardless of any evidence that there is a risk. I can only assume that this portrayal seeks to activate a fear based experience in the listener.

This is critically important because the information we take in has real effects on us. Unfortunately, we typically consume most of the information we are bombarded with unconsciously (and a lot of it is negative). Advertisers of course love this, as do politicians. The solution is to pay attention to what we consume, how much we consume and to spit out anything that "tastes" bad. Think of it like going to a food court in a mall. There is a wide variety of options. If you're conscious you can choose the healthier options most of the time. The second choice for living well then is to: choose to consume consciously most of the time.

Please don't use this principle to avoid any information that doesn't fit with your current beliefs. We do need to challenge our beliefs so that we don't narrow our view of what is possible, however, if the information doesn't nourish your spirit don't consume it. Basically, you need to consciously examine whether the information

> **TRY THIS: Evaluate what you consume**
>
> - Is the information credible and useful.
> - Who is providing the information. Identify their credentials.
> - Are they being objective.
> - Look for credible alternative views. Examine whether the information is up to date.
> - Determine if the information has positive practical value. Is it actionable?

coming at you is helpful or harmful to your well-being. The new knowledge may expand your perspective or be a call to action. However, it may also just promote a negative attitude that shrinks your life. Awareness is the key. If you are feeling stuck, pay attention to what you are consuming and consciously evaluate it.

As noted in the previous chapter, negative facts can be included in a positive view of reality. Shawn Achor highlights that successful people do not ignore negative facts. They do, however, attend to their capacity and resources to address those facts. They also look for other perspectives that offer life affirming information that can be used to help them move forward more effectively. There is a buffet of information to choose from. Choose wisely.

In addition to unplugging from negative consumption, it is important to plug into positive experiences. Neuropsychologist Rick Hanson notes that negative information makes linkages more quickly and easily in the brain due to the negativity bias. He suggests that we must, therefore, consciously look for and savour positive moments so that they too become integrated into the brain. Hanson suggests that taking 10 to 20 seconds to absorb positive information and experiences make them "stickier" neurologically and more likely to help us balance out the negative information that surrounded us.

To be most effective, it is important for the absorption to be a full mind-body experience. In other words, you must do more than think about the

> **TRY THIS: Savor the Positive**
>
> 1. Identify a positive experience: from your present experience, from the past or from a positive anticipation.
> 2. Write down what it is, name the emotion and how it feels in your body.
> 3. Absorb it by thinking, feeling and sensing it or 10-20 seconds.

positive experience, you must also feel it emotionally and sense it in the body. For example, how do your muscles feel when you are grateful? How about your organs? Do you feel warm or cool? In my own experience I feel a soft, warm and open sensation in my chest when I am focused on gratitude. My body is relaxed but with a straight posture and there is a gentle smile on my face.

To help people "feel" the positive experiences in their body, I sometimes have my clients practice with the body directly. For example, I ask them to smile and take a moment to sense how their face feels when they smile and notice what thoughts and emotions smiling evokes. Other times I have them practice shifting to a strong back (sitting or standing straight) and open heart (soft, relaxed, open chest) posture. Again, I get them to notice what feelings and thoughts are evoked from this posture compared to a tight restricted or collapsed posture.

Finally, keep in mind that you always consume what you put out. If you say negative things you consume them. If you speak positively, you consume that. As Miguel Ruiz pointed out in his book *The Four Agreements*, it is important to have integrity with our

> **TRY THIS: Speak Positively**
>
> - Pay someone a compliment
> - Tell someone how grateful you are that they are in your life
> - Encourage someone
> - Ask someone about what is going well for them
> - Identify and share what is working in a relationship or interaction
> - Use respectful language when you disagree

words because through words we express our intent and help co-create our lives. I encourage you to speak in ways that adds value to your life and to the people around you.

I would like to conclude this chapter with a story I heard some time ago from a First Nations elder. It is a story that perhaps you have heard as well. In this story a grandfather is talking to his grandson about how he feels. He says that he feels like he has two wolves fighting in his heart. One wolf is angry, resentful and negative. The other wolf is loving and compassionate. The grandson asks him which wolf will win the fight in his heart. The grandfather answers, "the one that I feed." It matters what you feed yourself. Pay attention to what information you are taking in, **choose what to consume and absorb life affirming information regularly.**

CHAPTER 3

HOW TO GET OUT OF A 10 FT HOLE

"Man can be tremendously happy or unhappy and he is free to choose. This freedom is hazardous. This freedom is dangerous – because you become responsible." Osho

HOW TO GET OUT OF A 10-FOOT HOLE

I'd like to start this chapter with a thought experiment. Imagine you fell down a 10-foot hole. Maybe you fell down that hole because someone pushed you in. Maybe you fell down that hole because you were curious about it and fell in as you were exploring. Maybe you just happened to be in the wrong place at the wrong time. A pure accident. How much time do you want to spend figuring out who is to blame for being in the bottom of the hole?

When I present this to clients, everyone immediately recognizes that figuring out who is to blame is a waste of time, because even if you are accurate, it will not get you out of the hole. Instead, what is important is to work on getting out. Yet in everyday life I see so many people whose lives are stuck because they insist on focusing on who is to blame for their life's problems.

As Osho pointed out in the quote at the beginning of the chapter, freedom only comes through responsibility. When I worked in the prison system, I used to say to the inmates that came to see me that the prison cells were not their only jail. A much bigger and fiercer prison was in their own minds. The bars of this prison were made of the beliefs they held regarding how they saw the world. These beliefs guided them into being stuck or trapped psychologically as well as physically.

One particularly damaging story we can all get caught up in is the story that others are to blame for our problems in life. If others are to blame then we are not responsible for changing our circumstances. It is a seductive story because what others do, can and does impact us[5]. Does this, however, mean that we are powerless?

As Viktor Frankle pointed out when discussing his experience as a concentration camp survivor, our ability to choose our attitude remains even when everything else is taken from us. It struck me as I was reading his story that if he can choose to be responsible for his conduct in that most oppressive of environments, then in the end, we all still have responsibility for how we choose to face our circumstances. Taking responsibility for ourselves does not abdicate other's responsibility for their actions but it does refocus our attention to the only place we can exert control – ourselves.

Bill, an inmate I worked with, was a perfect example of someone stuck in his own negative story and belief about the world. Bill had been in jail several times, mostly for stalking and domestic violence offences. He repeatedly shared stories regarding how his ex-wife and her family took advantage of him and set his life up for failure. He believed that they were the cause of his life problems and frequent prison sentences. When I asked him how long he was separated from his ex-wife he said twenty years….twenty years! I was astounded. Yet he still carried this resentment and he used it to keep himself stuck both in the past and in jail. This resentment was his excuse for not taking responsibility for his life.

This reminded me of a story I heard once from a

---

[5] The toughest belief barriers are the ones that include incomplete or partial truths.

Buddhist teacher and I shared this with Bill. There were two monks travelling from one monastery to another for a retreat. This order of monks had a prohibition against touching women. It had rained long and hard the night before their journey and the road ahead was often muddy and difficult to pass. At one such crossing they met a young attractive woman who was well dressed and studying how she might cross a rather large muddy section without ruining her dress. She was travelling to another town to meet her betrothed. The first monk, with her permission, picked her up and carried her across and then placed her down. The monks then continued their journey. The second monk did not say a thing. In fact, he did not speak again until they reached the monastery the following evening. The first monk asked him if everything was alright. He finally burst out saying that he has been troubled since the crossing and that he could not stop thinking about what happened. He finally asked the first monk how he could violate the rules of the order by picking up a woman. The first monk simply responded by saying, "I put her down yesterday, why are you still carrying her."

The moral of the story is that we often carry disturbing events in our minds, playing them over and over again even when the situation has long ended. We carry things with us long past their best before date. Bill was doing the same thing. I had no way of knowing whether he was treated unfairly but I did know that he was stuck because of how he chose to think about his life. He chose to keep his perception of the past hurts he suffered alive every day by how he chose to think about his life and the stories he chose to tell about his life. Remember we become what we consume and we consume the stories we share. He was keeping himself a prisoner by blaming his ex-wife for his situation. His path to freedom was taking responsibility for his actions and his life. He just couldn't see that yet because he could not distinguish between blame and responsibility.

Often when people come to see me for challenges in their lives they will tell me that they are willing to take some blame for their current circumstances but other people are also to blame. Common ways of saying this include, "it's a two-way street" or "it takes two to tango." I refer to this as the blame pie with my clients. To explain this, I typically draw a circle and put a line down the middle and write 50% blame in each half. People tend to nod in agreement. I then cross out the whole thing and draw two or more separate circles and write 100% in each circle. I then explain that we are all 100% responsible for our own choices and action. You are not responsible for another's choices but you are responsible for your own, including whether you react or respond appropriately to what you have experienced from others. Responsibility means you have the ability to respond. This is true even if you are in circumstances that other people created.

After four sessions with Bill repeating his story of blame despite my best efforts to help him shift focus, I decided we had to stop. At that moment, I did something unusual in therapy. In the fifth session after he once more began by blaming his ex-wife for his circumstances, I told him he needed to stop talking. I felt my stomach tightening and I was feeling nauseous. You see your body will give you clues if you are stuck.

The body's response to being stuck is constriction. I could feel how stuck he was and it was manifesting in my own body.

I suggested to Bill that if I was feeling constricted after listening to him share the same story four or five times, I could imagine how constricted he felt and I could see why he is so stuck. I suggested to him that he was so tight and tense that nothing could move or change in his life. I compassionately told him that he was emotionally constipated from holding on to a twenty-year grudge and that I was worried about how his life would proceed if he didn't learn how to let go and move on. I suggested to him that he needed an emotional enema. I also told him that I could not listen anymore to this story and needed him to leave my office because I was too constricted to help him that day. I did offer him the opportunity of returning the following week if he was willing to look at moving forward instead of backwards.

Bill did come back. He started his next session with a smile and asked me how he could get an emotional enema and if it hurts. Bill worked hard after that session and took responsibility for his life. My last knowledge of him was that he was living well and had not returned to old patterns. Taking responsibility can be difficult and can require a lot of energy but it is essential.

Blame on the other hand is easy, at least in the short term. Blame does not require much effort nor do you need to take any action to change your life. If others are responsible for your bad fortunes, then what can you do about it? You think, "They are the one's that must change not me." It's a great way to become a "victim" and give up choices in life. Like Bill, these kinds of "victims" can also be externally reactive and cause victimization in others as well. They will of course blame the other for their bad behaviour.

Blaming yourself, by the way, also does not help. Research shows that self-criticism doesn't lead to responsibility and change but rather to stress and anxiety. People tend to respond to stress and anxiety by using the same self-soothing, avoiding or reactive strategies for which they are criticizing themselves. Procrastinators will procrastinate more to feel better about feeling bad about procrastinating. Similarly, those who abuse alcohol or drugs will use more alcohol and drugs to feel better about feeling so bad about using alcohol and drugs. People who beat themselves up over not maintaining their diet when they are trying to lose weight tend to then overeat to deal with the stress of the self-criticism and shame of not sticking to their diet.

It turns out that self-compassion is much more effective than being tough on yourself. People who treat themselves kindly are more likely to take responsibility for their challenges and mistakes and make appropriate changes. They are also more likely to listen to feedback and use it to improve and move forward. In general, research shows that in states of compassion individuals tends to increase their sense of accountability and responsibility and engage in more positive behaviour.

Taking responsibility is less a skill we need to develop and more a natural occurrence when we let go of blame. Other people's behaviours and choices will of course have an impact on our lives, and sometimes a negative impact. We are not responsible for other people's negative choices, only for our response. One way to get away from the blame trap when dealing with other people's negative choices is through the practices of forgiveness and letting go.

To illustrate the simplicity of letting go, I get my clients to hold on to an object that represents their blame (or their resentments or their fears) out in front of them. I ask them to hold the object as tightly physically as they are holding the painful story emotionally and cognitively. We discuss how much effort that requires and how the longer they hold on the more energy it requires. Then I ask them to open their hand and let the object go. It is easy. It is effortless. It is freeing. It takes much more energy to hold on than to let go. We fear that we will drop into an abyss if we let go but instead we become, as Martin Luther King Jr. once said, "Free at last". When we let go of blame we naturally fall into responsibility.

There is nothing else left to do but to choose, to decide, to live.

TRY THIS: Letting Go

1. Name your intention to let go
2. Breathe in and name the feeling or experience you wish to release
3. Breathe out and say, "I let this go."
4. Repeat steps 2 and 3
5. Be gentle and patient. It doesn't all have to be released at once

The practice of letting go is **not about forgetting** what has happened **but of releasing** the pain and suffering that keeps us trapped in the past. The practice involves acknowledging the hurts we have experiences so that we can release them. If we try to deny them they will persist. Letting go can be tied to practices of forgiveness. Forgiveness, as Jack Kornfield once said is, "giving up hope for a better past." Wise forgiveness involves:

1. Letting go of past suffering and betrayal
2. Releasing pain and hatred
3. Courage
4. Seeing our mutual humanity

Wise forgiveness does NOT involve or require:
1. Forgetting or condoning
2. A continued relationship with those that have cause harm

It is also important to understand that you cannot rush forgiveness. It may not happen quickly.

As noted earlier, we also need to show compassion and forgiveness to ourselves. Kristin Neff has studied and written extensively on this topic. Self-compassion helps people thrive by encouraging more responsibility for their lives while suffering less anxiety and depression. Within this approach, negative emotions are not supressed but rather embraced and transformed. She has identified 3 components to self-compassion: self-kindness, mutual humanity and mindfulness. Within this perspective, we recognize the truth about ourselves, that as humans we are imperfect and that the world is imperfect. Consequently, failures and challenges are understood as part of life. In this way, we also recognize that we are not alone in this journey. We are all the same in experiencing opportunities and obstacles, successes and mistakes. Finally, we can recognise that negative thoughts and emotions can arise but we do not have to supress them or indulge in them. We can observe them without judgement Thus, we begin to understand our negative experiences but also that we are so much more that those experiences. In this larger frame, the emotions move and transform.

Further practices for working with self-compassion and letting go are offered in chapter nine. Another way to refocus on our responsibility is to attend to our own personal values. In other words, the principles that we hold regarding how we wish to treat ourselves and other people. I will explore this in more detail in chapter seven.

> **TRY THIS: Self-Compassion**
>
> 1. Acknowledge your own issue; name it
> 2. Acknowledge that this is a human experience. Say to yourself: "others have also experienced this."
> 3. Say to yourself:
>   a. May I give myself compassion
>   b. May I be kind to myself
>   c. May I forgive myself
>   d. May I be patient

In summary, responsibility is recognizing our ability to respond. It is an act of courageous living because it avoids the easy way out. It provides a great deal of freedom because we no longer allow ourselves to be a victim of other people's choices or our perception of their choices and actions. Certainly, we cannot escape being victimized from time to time in life, but even during those times we do not need to give up who we are and how we wish to live our life. The third choice for living well then is to **take responsibility for our actions.**

CHAPTER 4

LIKE RIDING A BIKE

"It is the same with people as it is with riding a bike. Only when moving can one comfortably maintain one's balance." Albert Einstein

LIKE RIDING A BIKE

Have you ever found yourself acting against your own long-term interest because you were tired or worn out? Maybe you ate that extra piece of pie, or you procrastinated another day on that project you needed to get done? Maybe you started an argument over something small and said things you later regretted or you acted impulsively in a way that might have felt good in the moment but that act had negative consequences for yourself and/or other people in your life?

A common example that many people have faced is the fight they have with family members when they are hungry. In popular culture, we call it being "*hangry*." There was even a popular award-winning chocolate bar commercial that played off this theme with the tag line, "you're not yourself when you're hungry."

I know that I have experienced this with both family and friends. One memorable event happened with my parents and brother while on a trip to Greece. Although all of us had been to Greece many times in the past, this was the first time since childhood that all four of us were there at the same time. My parents, therefore, wanted to take me and my brother on an extensive tour of the country of their birth since we were now at an age where we could appreciate the history and beauty that they saw.

On road trips, my father likes to start early and drive as long as he can until we get to our destination. I remember fondly, as a child living in Montreal, when in the summers, my parents would pack us in the car at two in the morning while half asleep. We would then drive down south for 6-8 hours going to Cape Cod or some other beach destination. My brother and I would fall asleep again for most of the journey and wake up with excitement as we were just arriving at our vacation spot.

In Greece, however, we were not children sleeping in the back seat but adults and the tour they had planned was a 5500 kilometer journey over seven days. Things were great when we arrived at our destinations but tensions in the automobile had built up. By the third day, bickering in the vehicle was common. As a newly trained psychologist, I took it upon myself to try to get my family members to calm down and breathe. I must have told them to stop and take a breath about 10 times a day while driving.

By the end of the sixth day I didn't realize how hungry and exhausted I was when we finally stopped for a late lunch. We had ordered and a small disagreement occurred between my parents where they had a different opinion about a historical event. I should note that these types of arguments are a bit of national past-time for Greeks and I have been known to partake in them myself from time to time.

On this day however, I must admit that being tired, hungry and spending too much time trying to care for everyone else's emotional needs but my own, I had little energy left for my own emotional regulation. I reacted with a verbal outburst stating among other things that I have had enough of the bickering (using more colourful language). I then stood up with such flourish that my chair fell backwards. The chair landed on the ground with a noticeably loud thud capturing the other patrons' attention. Finally, as everyone in the restaurant stared, I stormed out and started walking quickly down the street. After 10 minutes, I finally stopped and realized what I had done. By that time my family had left the restaurant and drove by to pick me up (I must have walked about one kilometer). I apologized for my behaviour and my father, with a smile, reminded me that breathing was important.

You see life takes energy. Overcoming challenges takes energy. Learning takes energy. Sticking with our long-term goals takes energy. Anytime we have to make a decision, filter out distractions, focus attention, or fight an impulse we use up energy. If we do not pay attention to our energy, we may find ourselves burned out or acting in ways that don't support our life.

Energy depletion does not mean that we lose control and it is not an excuse to avoid taking responsibility for our actions. When my clients offer these types of excuses or justifications I challenge them immediately. For example, regardless of how tired, hungry or angry we might be, we are still less likely to yell or hit some people (e.g., our boss or a police officer) and more likely to react with others (e.g., family members). So, we control ourselves with bosses because they can fire us but we may give ourselves permission to react with family and friends because we don't expect to get fired.

Looking at my own situation, you could see that I demonstrated control. I did not, for example, hit anyone nor did I break anything. I was still responsible for my actions both in terms of allowing myself to reach that level of energy depletion and in how I chose to react in that state. Energy depletion has very real neurological and psychological effects on us but it does not mean we lose control. We remain responsible for our actions.

Nevertheless, it is important to pay attention to our energy level because otherwise we risk burning out. In states of energy depletion, we are not at our best. Below is a list of symptoms of burnout or compassion fatigue. Look and see if any of them sound familiar.

- Irritation and dissatisfaction
- Increased negativity and pessimism
- Sleep and appetite disruption
- Preoccupation & difficulty concentrating
- Physical, emotional & mental exhaustion
- Feelings of hopelessness & helplessness in work & life
- Depression may occur – we become detached
- Personal and professional relationships begin to collapse

To understand burnout, we need to understand our brain. Our brain requires energy to operate properly. Additionally, our brain uses almost a quarter of the energy of the whole body. A large portion of that is in our frontal cortex, the area of our brain that we often refer to as our executive functioning. As Kelly McGonagall describes in her book *The Willpower Instinct*, that is the part of the brain that can help us say yes to what supports our lives, to say no to what will interfere with our lives and to keep our long-term interests in mind when faced with immediate gratification.

Energy depletion will have an impact on our frontal

cortex and consequently our resourcefulness. All of a sudden, our capacity to stay focused on our long-term goals goes down, as does our capacity to say no to choices that may interfere with our long-term good (but may feel good right now). We are now more likely to be reactive to our environment rather than responsive. We are more likely to give ourselves permission to follow base impulses (e.g., eat too much of the wrong thing, have an adult tantrum, etc.) than consider the consequences of those actions for our long-term good.

The good news is that we can address this problem quite simply by being more aware of our energy levels and rebalancing our system as is necessary throughout the day. There are five key factors associated with energy balance: good sleep, exercise, proper nutrition, periodic recharging and creating healthy boundaries so that we do not over extend ourselves. This rebalancing is a dynamic experience. Because life can be unpredictable in its demands, it is important that we pay attention and adjust each of these five areas on an ongoing basis.

Unfortunately, all too often people tell me that they will catch up on their sleep on the weekend or rest on their holidays but do very little to manage their energy on a regular basis. I hear people saying that they will get to meditation or exercise when they find the time. I often wonder where they will find this time. Most people only get between 2-4 weeks of holidays a year. At best, that is less than 8% of your life. Weekends represent about a quarter of our life but we often have chores to do on weekends as well. Playing catch-up and looking for extra magical time is a recipe for burnout.

Sleep deprivation has significant negative effects on our health and impacts both cognitive and physical performance. Sleep deprivation can be a safety concern in professions where reaction times and decision making is critical (e.g., drivers, medical personnel). Maintaining good sleep hygiene is important for sustaining a healthy and regular sleep schedule. In general, adults need 7-8 hours of sleep per night whereas teenagers require 9 hours and infants up to 16 hours of sleep. For difficulties falling asleep, Simon Fraser University researcher Luc Beaudoin has developed the "cognitive shuffle" technique that appears to be effective in helping shut off an overactive mind. The technique involves prompting users to imagine various objects or scenes in rapid succession thus simulating the process of falling asleep.

> **TRY THIS: Sleep Hygiene Tips:**
>
> - Create a relaxing sleep environment.
> - Don't discuss or deal with stressful or anxiety-inducing situations right before bedtime.
> - Set a sleep schedule.
> - Limit naps.
> - Maintain a regular exercise routine.
> - Avoid late night meals and alcohol consumption.
> - Curb nicotine and caffeine use.
> - Schedule down time before bed.
> - Don't check the clock.

We also know that regular physical exercise is one of the best ways to boost our energy levels. Energy creates more energy. Many experts recommend about

150 hours of moderate activity per week. It may help to aim for 30 minutes of exercise daily. Children and youth require at least 60 minutes of daily activity. Exercise also helps us sleep better and improves our mood. Please consult your doctor before beginning an exercise program, especially if you have a medical condition.

Furthermore, research shows that small breaks throughout the day will boost our energy levels and consequently improve our creativity and productivity. Even five minutes of meditation or time in nature acts as an energy balancer. This is because our energy is a finite but renewable resource. It is therefore important to incorporate activities that will give us small boosts throughout the day. It turns out that my "taking a breath" advise to my family was indeed useful. If only I had practiced what I was preaching.

> **TRY THIS: Simple Recharges**
>
> Spend 5 minutes in nature or meditating every day and as needed
>
> Imagine you are in a pleasant environment for a few minutes.
>
> Keep healthy snacks around to maintain your blood sugar level
>
> Train your brain:
>
> 1. Use your non-dominant hand for two weeks
> 2. Visualize accomplishing your goal

Fueling with nutrition is also critically important. We need to remember to eat when we are hungry, with healthy energy dense food so that we are not "running on fumes." Research shows that the brain uses blood glucose levels as indicator of energy in the body. If blood glucose levels are consistently dropping our brain will go into conservation mode. A low glycemic index diet appears to be appropriate from an energy perspective because it focuses on how foods affect our blood sugar levels.

It turns out that we can also strengthen our frontal cortex and energy system with training. Athletes push their capacities by challenging their bodies but not overwhelming them. For example, if you want to be stronger through weight training, you begin to train with weights that will work your muscle but that are not so heavy that you injure yourself. In the same way, we can strengthen our frontal cortex by training our attention. A simple technique involves using your non-dominant hand for two weeks for opening doors, brushing your teeth and drinking water. Researchers have found that this simple exercise can improve self control for eating and managing behaviour. This task requires us to use some but not a lot of energy to focus. So, like proper weight training it helps improve our capacity to focus long-term without overwhelming us. Furthermore, we can train by using our imagination. Your brain treats imagination like reality. So, you can visualize being in a calm relaxed space and you will relax and re-charge. You can also visualize accomplishing your goals and your brain will activate your prefrontal cortex to help you stay focused.

The final lesson on energy balance involves understanding how to preserve energy[6] through

---

[6] We can also leak energy through anxiety created by focusing on things we cannot change or consuming the wrong things. We can create boundaries on what we consume and we can gently re-orient our attention to where our energy is most

boundaries. Adam Grant in his book *Give and Take* discusses research on three types of people: Givers, Takers and Matchers. *Givers*, are the generous compassionate individuals who try to help others with no strings attached. *Takers*, are the type of people who give very little but try to take as much as possible for themselves. I refer to them as psychological vampires. They will suck your energy dry if you let them. Finally, there are the *Matchers*. They operate under the principle of reciprocity. They believe in fairness and equality in giving and taking. You can refer to this style as the "you scratch my back and I'll scratch your back" attitude to life.

When looking at who were the top and bottom performers in a variety of occupations and industries (e.g., medicine, sales, engineering) the results were the same. Which group do you think ended up at the bottom? What about the top? It turns out that Givers represented the majority of both the worst performers and the best performers. So, nice people finish last but they also finish first. The question then becomes what distinguishes successful givers from failed givers? The answer, in my reading of the research, is simple. Successful givers also had boundaries. They saw themselves in

> **TRY THIS: Create Healthy Boundaries**
>
> Say yes to yourself and what is important first.
>
> Ask what is best for everyone, including yourself, and act from that perspective.
>
> Practice self-compassion

---

useful. The first two chapter addressed these issues.

the circle of care and, therefore, they did not give to the point of exhaustion and burnout. Failed givers would not say no and eventually would get burned out. Takers love these kinds of no boundary givers and will frequently take advantage of them.

In my experience, these results carry over to all areas of our lives. Givers without boundaries get taken advantage of by others in their personal lives as well as their professional lives. They consequently suffer both physical and emotional breakdowns.

One of my clients was in an abusive relationship. Without clear boundaries, she had a hard time identifying the emotional abuse she was experiencing.[7] Even after leaving the abusive relationship she had a difficult time saying no to others. This frequently left her feeling overwhelmed and exhausted with little time for her own recovery or goals. Initially she even spent a great deal of time and energy worrying about and trying to help her abusive ex-partner. Eventually she learned that it was easier if she started saying yes to herself first. She would then say yes to others only when she had time and energy left over. Re-balancing her energy by including herself in the equation of need allowed her to be healthier and more effective in her life and work. She began to find and take on wonderful

---

[7] Regardless of boundary issues, a person victimized in a relationship is not responsible for the abuse they experience. Only the person engaging in the abusive acts is responsible for those acts. Additionally, there are many complex reasons women stay in abusive relationship including the fact that the risk of more severe abuse and physical violence increases when they attempt to leave an abusive relationship. There are many useful resources in communities where you can find information and support to understand and exit abusive relationships. There are also programs and services for offenders to help them take responsibility for their lives and end the cycle of violence (see the source notes for links to these resources).

opportunities that helped her grow as an individual even as she contributed to the betterment of her community. She is now on her way to becoming a successful giver.

It is important to recognize that part of my client's journey in creating boundaries and rebalancing her energy involved developing compassion for herself. To get her to look at compassion more broadly, I shared this moral dilemma story I heard once about a group of monks.

In this story, the monks decided to head out on a retreat together. There was the head monk, a monk that was his best friend, a very old monk, a very sick monk (who was near death), a lazy monk who didn't always do his fair share, an annoying monk who disagreed with everyone about everything and a very young monk who had not yet achieved much knowledge or wisdom. The monks found a cave for their retreat and settled in only to be discovered by a group of bandits who were planning to use that same cave. The leader of the bandits wanted to kill the monks but monks are very good at talking. The head monk convinced the bandits not to kill them on the promise that they would remain silent about the bandits. The leader of the bandits however indicated that one of the monks needed to be killed to show that the bandits meant business and that there would be consequences if they were betrayed. He gave the leader of the monks one hour to choose who would be killed. Whom did he choose?

Most people, especially givers, will say he chose himself. This is what my client said when I presented her with the story. Self-sacrifice is a common trait of givers, especially burned out givers. When I say this is incorrect, people usually try to get logical and assume that it is either the sick or old monks who are near death anyways. Some, for reasons you can probably guess at, will say the annoying or lazy monk. The answer, however, is that the leader monk would not choose. His compassion was equal for all including himself. Thus, there was no choice that could be made.

My client needed to see that she was just as worthy of care and compassion as others and that compassion for herself did not diminish her kind and generous spirit but enhanced it. Practices in self compassion helped and they can be quite simple as previously discussed. It is also important to remember that rebalancing your energy does not happen once and it is done. Like Einstein says in the opening quote, balance is like riding a bike. It is only achieved in motion. As we move in life we can make adjustments, take time to ground and replenish, acknowledge errors in ourselves and others and practice compassion and forgiveness.

In conclusion, remember to **choose to keep your energy balanced on a regular basis** as you move through life. Be aware of the five factors that play a role in maintaining and managing your energy levels. Are you getting enough sleep and exercise? Are you eating well and regularly? Do you take appropriate breaks to recharge your batteries? Are you maintaining appropriate boundaries so you are not leaking energy or being bled dry? Make choices that keep your energy balanced and you will find the energy to meet the demands of your life and to pursue your goals.

CHAPTER 5

LEMONADE, FERTILIZER and the ART of REFRAMING

"Just when the caterpillar thought that the world was over it became a butterfly." English Proverb

LEMONADE, FERTILIZER and the ART of REFRAMING

Alchemy is the art of turning one thing into another. In ancient times, there was a belief that you can transmute a common substance of little value (for example, lead), into something of great value (for example, gold). In his famous book the *Alchemist*, Paulo Coelho, speaks to the psychological elements of alchemy as involving the transformation of the person. Similarly, Tara Bennet-Goleman in her book *Emotional Alchemy* suggests that the true meaning of alchemy is that we all have the natural ability to turn our moments of confusion into insight and clarity.

One of the most powerful psychological experiences we can engage in, is the act of transforming our moments of pain and difficulty to resources or opportunities. Through this transformation we can then engage in the world in a different and more effective way. In psychology, we often refer to this alchemy as reframing. In everyday language, we talk about turning lemons into lemonade or the crasser metaphor of turning manure into fertilizer so that out of something negative, growth and beauty is possible.

This is more common than you might think. Research in psychology has shown that between 30% and 70% of people report positive changes after encountering personal suffering. Positive psychology practitioners and researchers refer to this as post-traumatic growth in recognition of the fact that we can also grow in significant ways from pain, trauma and other life challenges.

Reframing is not easy and it can take time. It can, however, be powerful. One of my clients experienced a wonderful reframe that shifted his focus from suffering to renewal. It did not change his circumstances but it relieved him of some significant suffering and consequently he could put more energy into his healing.

He is a medical doctor from an African country who immigrated to Canada to begin a new life. He was a well-established medical practitioner in Africa and held some prestigious positions. Nevertheless, like many professional immigrants into North America, he needed to prove his equivalency in competency to our College of Physicians and Surgeons and this required him to take courses and exams. Consequently, he was working in menial positions while getting his equivalency.

Unfortunately, one evening while driving home, he was rear-ended by another vehicle whose driver was distracted by being on her phone. The accident happened as he was waiting to merge on the highway and his vehicle was hit so hard it almost pushed him unto oncoming traffic just as an eighteen-wheel truck was speeding by. At that moment, he believed that he might die.

In addition to the psychological trauma, he also suffered physical injuries including migraines, and other pain in his neck and shoulders. This affected his ability to read and concentrate which of course affected his ability to complete his equivalency. He began to wonder if he would ever be able to return to medicine and he began to feel great sadness at this potential loss and great anger towards the distracted driver.

In our work together, several things became clear. First, he strongly identified with being a medical doctor. For him this meant being a caring person who attempts to save people's lives or at least improve their lives. He was also carrying a lot of resentment and anger towards the distracted driver. This was causing guilt as it was inconsistent with his sense of self as a compassionate person. His resentment also took a lot of his energy and he reported that he thought about that person daily. Finally, his thoughts were also consumed by the fact that he could have died. He had flashbacks of the truck speeding by so close to his vehicle as he was pushed forward. These thoughts and images disturbed his sleep further diminishing his concentration and increasing his tension and pain.

One session it dawned on me that he saved her life. I asked him what would have happened to her if he was not in front of her on the entrance to the highway? He realized that, distracted as she was, she would have driven straight into the oncoming traffic and likely been killed by the truck. We discussed how he in fact saved her life. That his presence saved her life. Therefore, even though he wasn't practicing medicine yet in Canada, he was still saving lives.

This reframe shifted something for him. His body became lighter and he could let go of his resentment and anger. This didn't mean he was letting go of his legal claim against her, there were still consequences for her distracted driving. Nevertheless, he could release his resentment and some of his trauma for his own safety. You see in his medical practice in Africa he would occasionally put himself in danger in the performance of his duties. The risk he experienced in this context was, therefore, also reframed as part of saving a life.

Having freed up energy from resentment and trauma he could focus more on his physical recovery and his future. He regained momentum for moving forward with his goals once more. The path ahead was still full of challenges but he was no longer contributing to those challenges by being stuck mentally and emotionally. This renewed understanding was a pivotal moment in his healing. Keep in mind that post-traumatic growth does not mean that we do not suffer after reframing or that the trauma isn't harmful and distressing. It does, however, allow us to find the resources and strength to move through the struggle more effectively.

Frames are, therefore, very important. A frame is a way in which we see the world. You can think of it as a belief or a perspective that we use to understand the world. It sets the boundaries of how we see the world much in the same way that a picture frame sets the boundaries of the picture. What is outside of the frame is not visible to us. Having a specific frame is not a problem in and of itself. It is only when the frame we are using is not working for us or when we are so inflexible that we do not see other ways of looking at the world.

Perhaps you have heard of the story of the three blind men and the elephant. One man felt the leg of the elephant and believed the elephant was a sturdy tree. Another man felt the elephant's trunk and believed it was a snake, while the third man felt the ear and believed it was a rug. By examining only one part of the elephant they could not understand the true nature of an elephant. In the same way when we do not examine our perspectives we may be blind to important aspects of our reality.

Reframing involves stepping back and considering alternative frames and perspectives. There are many ways to reframe. A personal experience of reframing that was profound for me came to me during meditation. The challenge I was facing was significant anxiety over my invitation to appear on a television show discussing issues of domestic violence. Initially I was very excited about being invited to be the expert psychologist. You can imagine this was a boost to my ego. (Move over Dr. Phil, here comes Dr. Harry). The night before my appearance however I could not sleep. I kept thinking "what if I forget everything I know and say something dumb." I worried that if I did that my career would be ruined. My anxiety was through the roof.

I decided to get up and meditate. As I became centered and calmed down, my mind and body opened. In that open state, a thought arose that changed everything. That thought was "it's not about you it's about the work." At that moment, all my stress disappeared. The television appearance was not about me or my success or my ego. Rather it was about providing a service to my community. It was about helping end domestic violence. This reframe from "it's about my success or expertise" to "it's about the work" was magical. For me this was gold. I continue to use this new frame whenever I am invited to speak publicly and my ego gets in the way. You too can reframe many of your negative views or the negative views that surround you. By changing the frame, we change what is visible and thereby also what is possible for how we move forward in our lives. [8]

Take for example the perspective that my friend and colleague Peter Levesque, president of the Institute for Knowledge Mobilization, has created around competition. During one conversation we discussed how many people get stuck in limiting competitive frames by comparing themselves to others. Peter observed how this framing can become a race to the bottom because people are trying to step over each other to "win." He noted, that in his experience, many people get stuck in this frame when looking at someone else's success because they think and act with the perspective of "I want what you have." This often turns to envy and a win/lose mindset. From this perspective, they seek to sabotage the other and often hurt themselves in the process.

Peter told me that he prefers to view life form a different perspective. Instead of "I want what you have" he thinks, "I want to know how you got there so I can achieve what I want as well." This different frame changes the focus from envy to curiosity, from judgement to learning and from hopelessness to action. It is a shift from "what" to "how" and a change in energy from a defeating win/lose mentality (a takers mentality) to a creative and energized win/win mentality (i.e., a successful giver).

Reframing can be extremely difficult but it can also be quite simple and even small reframes can have profound impacts. One client, who was working

---

[8] The exercises discussed in chapter one on perspective taking can be tremendously useful if you are feeling stuck in your current frame.

towards reconciliation with his wife, noted that thinking about "getting back together" created anxiety for both him and his wife. They both had visions that the old patterns would resurface. I suggested that the problem was the word "back" and instead suggested they think about how to "move forward together." This change opened their perspective to what was possible and what they wanted to create rather than what they were afraid might happen.

Changing frames can also involve shifting the focus of a group of people in a setting. Another client I was seeing for anger management problems at work, reported that the constant conversations about the unfair demands of management and the poor labour relations were having a negative impact on him. He would go to work and hear stories about the latest unfairness and he would start seething immediately. He noted that almost all the conversations at work were about what was going wrong with labour relations. Unfairness and injustice were the most common conversations. When he came to see me, he was on stress leave. After helping him learn several self-regulation tools, he was coping better and we began planning his gradual return to work. At this point he became worried that becoming inundated with the stories of unfairness at work would bring him back to where he was before his stress leave. We discussed reframing his environment. Can you imagine how we could do that?

In this case I suggested that the environment was being framed by the conversations. He and his co-workers were only sharing stories about work problems. I suggested that he start conversations with his co-workers that were about what is going well for them. This changed the tone of many of the conversations to being about positive life and work experiences and this balanced out the negative experiences. My client was surprised at how well this worked.

Research by Barbara Fredrickson has shown that when you activate 3 positive experiences for every negative one you move your life from one that is floundering to one that is thriving. In fact, this positive framing is how I begin most of my therapy sessions with clients. The first question I ask after the initial assessment session is "What is better this week?" The question frames the mind to look for improvements so that new healthier possibilities become visible.

The process of reframing can be difficult, especially when people are dealing with significant suffering from a serious medical (e.g., illness or disease) or social issue (e.g., abuse and trauma). Be patient with yourself and be willing to seek help. Remember from the earlier chapters, we are not looking to deny negative realities but rather to add perspectives that can be more useful. As Terry White, a former envoy for the Archbishop of Canterbury noted after surviving five years of imprisonment by Hezbollah, "Suffering is universal but we can also turn that suffering around so that it becomes a positive force."

> **TRY THIS: Reframe your environment**
>
> Start conversation with what is going well
>
> Ask friends, family and co-workers to share their positive experiences.

Journaling can help. Explore and respond to questions that seek to open your view regarding how you are seeing your current circumstances.

> **TRY THIS: Journaling for Reframing**
>
> - How have you become sensitized to the pain of others through this problem?
> - Is there anything you could do to make the world a better place or reduce the likelihood of others will suffer as you have?
> - How do you think this might fit into the bigger picture of your life?
> - Can you think of past traumas or problems that led you to a better place and that seem like necessary experiences when you look back on them now?
> - Do you think what you are going through right now could be one of those experiences?
> - Without being dismissive of your suffering, I was wondering if you think there was any lesson you have learned from this experience?
> - How do you think your life is better because of this problem even though you would not have chosen it?
> - What do you think you could contribute to the world or other people now that you have gone through this difficult time?

The fifth choice for living well is to **reframe problems into opportunities.**

CHAPTER 6

TRICKSTERS, BOXES and POSSIBILITIES

"The trickster's function is to break taboos, create mischief, stir things up. In the end, the trickster gives people what they really want, some sort of freedom." Tom Robbins

TRICKSTERS, BOXES and POSSIBILITIES

In one of my practicums in graduate school I was evaluating potential wellness instructors for an employee assistance program. It was a great gig. In my evaluation of these professionals I had an opportunity to learn and experience various wellness ideas and initiatives.

In one of these exploration, I did this guided visualization exercise with a potential instructor whereby I was opening to an inner guide. In my case, the imagery of the guide kept changing from human like to various animal representations. In my visualization, the guide identified itself as the trickster archetype saying that it has many names and many forms. I asked for advice moving forward in my life and the "guide" said, "Harry you will succeed in most of your endeavors, but frequently you will do things the hard way and it won't be easy for you." That response startled me out of the visualization.

The response had a profound impact on me and I remember reflecting on it from time to time as I moved forward in my life and career. I realized that in many ways I was indeed living the truth of that statement. I had many great successes in my life and career and yet I also noticed significant obstacles and challenges in many situations. I often took on roles and responsibilities that were rewarding but added undo stress and obstacles in my path. Additionally, I was blocked in accomplishing some of my life goals. One of those goals was writing a book.

About ten years later, I was involved with the

Canadian Society of Clinical Hypnosis (BC Division) as a board member and faculty. In this context, I had an opportunity not only to teach but to learn from eminent individuals in the field. In one of our education sessions, I sat in on a process my colleague Dr. Lee Pulos was conducting on overcoming barriers in achieving one's goals. During this process, the memory of the trickster message came back again and I decided I needed to explore this more fully. During the session, I engaged in a visualization where I reconnected with the trickster and asked him why it had to be difficult for me. In typical trickster fashion, he responded with, "oh you took that seriously, I was only kidding about that part." Then he laughed and I was out of the visualization and back in the room exasperated and then also laughing.

I had of course been my own trickster. After a bit more work on myself I realized that I carried a family and cultural mythology that life was difficult and I projected that out in my life. By accepting the belief, I lived it more often than was necessary. By becoming conscious that it is a belief I project into my life I have been able to notice more often when the challenges I face are part of my own creation and to stop getting in my own ways as often as I can. There are enough real obstacles and challenges in the world without having to create more.

Our beliefs about the world have real effects on our lives. Take for example the placebo and nocebo effect. Certain beliefs about treatment effects whether positive or negative will have real implications on individuals regardless of whether the drug or intervention is real. For example, during World War II, doctors were running out of morphine so instead of morphine many soldiers received a saline solution. Dr. Henry K. Beecher reported that these soldiers still experienced pain relief. In 1955, he published an article in the Journal of the American Medical Association outlining how placebos could be used to determine the effectiveness of medical treatments. Today, to prove a medicine is effective, pharmaceutical companies need to demonstrate effectiveness beyond what a placebo effect would be.

Although often seen as fake outcomes, placebo results not only include people reporting that they feel better but have been shown to stimulate real physiological responses. Some of the physiological changes measured include changes in heart rate, blood pressure and chemical activity in the brain. These results should not be interpreted to mean that we can believe our way into any change. Placebo effects typically offer real symptom relief and can be very effective with some conditions but can have no physical impact on other diseases. Nevertheless, they do demonstrate that how we look at the world, the beliefs and expectations we hold, can have real and profound implications on our lives.

Studies on stress further highlight how important beliefs are to health and performance and this even includes beliefs about stress. Health psychologist Kelly McGonigal refers to an eight-year study that tracked 30,000 adults that highlighted this fact. In this study, researchers found that mortality was not linked to the amount of stress a person experienced but to their belief about whether stress was good or bad for them. People that believed stress was helpful did well regardless of the amount of stress they reported experiencing.

It turns out that stress is necessary for a healthy life even if too much stress that is unmanaged can be detrimental. Studies at Yale University have demonstrated that changing people's belief about stress by highlighting the positive real aspects of stress changed how stress affected these individuals in laboratory settings. People introduced to the positive aspects of stress before being put under pressure felt more confident, less anxious, less fatigue and had fewer negative physiological signs of stress while concurrently showing a healthier cardiovascular profile.

What we believe can expand or place limits on our capacities to act in the world. Dr. Carol Dweck has studied mindsets of success and failure and notes that there is great power in believing that you can improve. She refers to this belief as a growth mindset. In her research, she noted that some children dealt with difficult challenges with a sense of judgment and failure. She referred to this as a fixed mindset because the belief held by these children is that change or growth is not possible or likely. On the other hand, the students with the growth mindset had a sense of challenge and possibility. In brain imaging studies of children, scientist have discovered that students with fixed mindsets had little activity in their brains when faced with a challenge. The students with a growth mindset however, had significant brain activity as they became fully engaged.

In her excellent TED talk Dr. Dweck refers to a school in Chicago who mobilized this knowledge to help their students succeed. Instead of giving failing grades the school gave a "Not Yet" grade to students who did not pass. The implication of "Not Yet" of course, is that success is just around the corner. It was a change of mindset from failure to possibility.

Fixed mindsets and limiting beliefs can also be cultural in nature impacting groups of people at the same time. One example of a broader belief having real implications on action involves how many cultures deal with anger. In my anger management groups, I frequently ask participants to tell me what they believe anger is. Typical responses involve descriptions of aggression (e.g., yelling, hitting), physiological symptoms that look aggressive (e.g., red face) or explosive metaphors (e.g., anger is like a volcano). When I playfully ask people to tell me what animal best represents anger, I do not get bunny rabbits and kittens. Instead people typically respond with such animals as tigers and sharks. When I ask, what colour represents anger, they typically respond with red or black. When I ask why, people will say because you can't see well when angry (things are black) or red for representing blood or the colour that insights bulls to charge in aggression. The animal representations of course reflect beliefs that anger is unpredictable and dangerous. These conceptions suggest that we must supress our experience of anger because it is dangerous but also that we will eventually fail in this suppression and explode into aggressive dangerous behaviour.

Although there are real neuro-biological effects to emotional experiences that influences how we express our emotions, emotions are more than specific behavioural patterns. Anger cannot be simply described as aggressive behaviour. In simple terms, emotions represent our experience of the world and provide energy to address these experiences. For example, sadness reflects our experience of loss and moves us to address that experience of loss. This can include being moved to tears or being moved to reach out for support. People may also engage in drinking or using drugs in order to hide or run from their pain. There is no necessary behaviour that must be performed when experiencing sadness though some choices are clearly healthier and more constructive than others.

Similarly, anger does not lead to just one kind of behavioural response. We all know from our own experiences and observations, situations where responses to being angry can vary from aggressive behaviour to passive behaviour to assertive responses. We know that a person angry with their boss may respond in one way but the same person may express anger to their children or their spouse in completely different ways. In some situations, individuals may respond to experiences of anger with maturity and in other situations use anger to justify their use of aggression.

Anger cannot be defined by behaviour. Instead we experience anger when we perceive unfairness. Without anger we would not address injustices in the world. It is an essential emotion. The belief that it involves aggression is the problem. This belief does not cause people to behave aggressively when angry but it does make visible and plausible certain ways of being when angry (reactive, aggressive, loud) and make other ways of being less visible and less plausible (assertive, calm, responsive). By recognizing that anger is not confined to a single pattern of behaviour we can stop giving ourselves permission to react aggressively when we are angry and to open ourselves to constructive responses to unfairness. One way to open our mindset involves opening our hearts.

Take, for example, one client I was working with for anger management issues. He came to see me primarily because his wife threatened to leave if he did not stop his controlling and demanding behaviours when he became angry. After a couple of months of therapy, he reported that his home life had much improved and that he no longer reacted aggressively with his family when he was angry. This was confirmed by his wife who was very pleased with the changes at home. One winter day, however, he came into the office all red and angry and so agitated that it looked like he was going to jump out of his own skin. He had gloves on and he took them off and slammed them on the table between us and offered me a challenge. He explained that his employees had done something wrong and then proceeded to tell me how in anger he had become threatening and verbally abusive to them and that they deserved it. He then dared me to identify any different way that he could have handled that situation given what they had done.

Do you think that he would have heard me if I have offered him healthy and respectful alternatives to what he had done? I did not think so either. So instead of answering his question I suggested that we come back to his question after we settle into our session with a simple exercise. I asked him to close his eyes and focus on someone he loves dearly. He focused on his son. I asked him to really feel the love for his son that he carries with him. To sense it in his body and to breathe into it. I noticed his breathing deepened and his facial, neck and shoulder muscles relaxed. After about a minute of being in that state I asked him to look back at the situation at work and ask himself if there was any other way he could have handled that situation. He smiled deeply and said "I get it. Yes." He then proceeded to tell me what he could have done and what he will do to take responsibility for his inappropriate behaviour while still holding his employees accountable for their actions.

You see, we mostly have our own answers and they are readily available to us, that is when we open and access our intelligence and wisdom. Please note that when he was asked think back to the situation at work while in the open state, the same inappropriate behaviour by his staff was recalled. He was still angry. His relationship to the unfairness, however, had changed.

To free ourselves from these fixed mindsets, we need to challenge our beliefs and we need to open our own mind and heart. It is only in opening that we can see possibilities. Creativity and adaptability requires opening first to access new options,

> **TRY THIS: Emotional Reset**
>
> Focus on someone you care for deeply
>
> Feel the emotion in your body as you think about this person
>
> Once you feel the emotional reset, look at the troubling situation again from this more open perspective and note what new options are available

then narrowing our focus to put new ideas into action. Without opening ourselves up we simply recreate old patterns. In some cases, these patterns are not a problem, in others they are limiting and potentially destructive.

When I teach workshops and seminars I frequently give this brain teaser to emphasize this point:

> Connect all 9 dots with 4 straight lines. You cannot however lift your pen off the 2-dimensional space and you cannot retrace over the same line.

● ● ●

● ● ●

● ● ●

Try this for a few minutes before turning to the end of the chapter for the solution.

If you didn't solve this problem don't feel badly. Most people do not solve this when they first see it and mostly for the same reason. What typically happens is that people create a square or a box in their mind when they see the 9 dots and then try to solve the problem within that mindset. The brainteaser is typically used to teach the "think outside the box" lesson. I, however, usually say there is no box. We created the box and we have trapped ourselves in our own creation. Like in life, the problem is real but the barrier to the solution is our belief about the problem, not the problem itself. It is the same with anger. Anger makes visible the reality of injustice. A significant barrier to dealing with the challenge of injustice constructively, however, is the belief we hold about anger. This is true of so many challenges we face.

We will all get caught up in these fixed mindsets at times. When we don't see possibilities, we need to ask ourselves whether we are in a box of our own creation. Then, we can look to shift our mindset. One way to do so is to talk to others to get a different view point. This does not have to be a professional. I will, however, offer one piece of advice when looking to others to get a different perspective. Don't look for opening from people who are in a smaller box than you. You can recognize these people because they sound something like," you think that is bad...let me tell you how bad things really are..."

Of course, like the client I referred to above, you can also engage in exercises that open your heart and mind. A focus on love and gratitude increases your heart rate variability, tones down your brain's alarm center and opens higher cortical functioning. You basically have more access to your own intelligence and wisdom.

TRY THIS: Priming a Growth Mindset

When stuck:

Practice gratitude to shift your emotional state

Slow down your breathing to 5-6 breathes per minute to increase your HRV and improve brain function

Add "not yet" to obstacles you have not overcome

Activate curiosity

Finally, you can mobilize the knowledge form Dr. Dweck's research by using the power of "Yet". A simple way to change our mindset and get out of the limits of our "boxed" in beliefs is to add the words "yet" to the challenge.

For example, every time you hear a voice (your own or someone else's) saying you are not ___ (e.g., good at this) add the word yet. I am not ___ yet. If you do not succeed add the word yet. I did not succeed yet. Notice the difference that makes in your experience. "I have not written a book." "I have not written a book yet." The first statement is a conclusion and has a sense of finality. The second statement has a sense of possibility and implies future action. There are many ways to shift to using language of possibility. For example, in reference to goals not quite achieved you can say this is where I have got to "so far." "So Far" similarly implies more progress is imminent.

In conclusion, when you are face to face with "the trickster," look in the mirror and examine your beliefs. If you can, laugh, then seek to learn the lesson in front of you. Being stuck can be frustrating and uncomfortable but it is also an opportunity. By opening your mindset, you build your capacity to grow and adapt. You become more resilient to future challenges and you gain freedom to pursue your goals and dreams.

The sixth choice for living well is **to open your mindset and look for possibilities in every situation.**

Solution to Brainteaser:

Solution – Open mindset

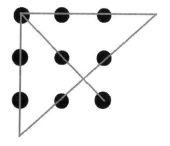

Closed mindset

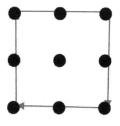

CHAPTER 7

LIVING the DASH

"It is good to have an end to journey toward; but it is the journey that matters, in the end." Ursula K. Le Guin

LIVING the DASH

My wife shared with me that when she was working in oncology dealing with life and death on a regular basis, the nurses often discussed how people choose to "live their dash." The dash represents the time and space between your year of birth and your year of death. You frequently see the dash on tombstones or obituaries. What counts is how you live that dash. The moment to moment choices you make, especially regarding how you interact with others. For the patients in oncology, the dash becomes even more important after diagnosis. With their mortality in the foreground, how they chose to live now becomes a vital consideration. We should not, however, wait until we are faced with our mortality to think about how we are living.

Some years ago, I was working with a very successful business man who came to see me at his wife's request. As he began telling me about his life he shared a series of successful achievements. He spoke of his success in school, his first job, his first promotion, his first car, his marriage, his first luxury car, his perfect house, his next promotion, his first million dollars and so on. After these series of accomplishments, I asked him if he was happy. Can you guess his answer? It was neither yes nor no. He said "Well, I should be." You see he came to see me because his wife threatened to leave and his daughter, when he came home early one day (a rare event for him), said to him "oh you came home early to see the new car not us." Ouch!

He had fallen into the trap many people do. He confused his goals with his life and financial success for happiness. The truth is that goals are essential and wealth is useful. Research, however, shows that it is not wealth that increases happiness but connection (more on this in the next chapter). What about achievement? This is more complicated in some ways because the problem isn't in having goals or pursuing goals; it is the idea that our happiness is proportionally related to our success.

During the Olympics in 1996 there was a commercial billboard that said: *"You Don't Win Silver – You Lose Gold."* The idea that you are either first or lumped in with everyone else as last persisted and this saying or its variations are still used today. In 2012 Australian Olympic silver medalist, Michell Watt, was asked about how disappointed he felt about coming short at the competition. His response was a challenge to the gold or bust, win at any cost mentality. He said, *"All the sports are becoming extremely competitive and more globalized. There are 210 countries here and if people can't realize that a silver medal is a great achievement then there's something wrong with them."* Think about the effect of the win at any cost ideology for the Olympics and competitive sports in general, it often leads to athletes risking their lives to take performance enhancing drugs.

This reference has also made it into other fields including business. For example, in a 2015 news conference the CEO of Oracle, Safra Catz, said, "This is how we feel: silver medal is the first loser" in referring to her company holding the number 2 slot in the business application market. If we take this mentality seriously then we are a planet of losers and the pursuit of absolute success can lead to all manner of sin. Do you remember the greed and shenanigans that led to the global financial crisis of 2008? With this philosophy, we focus less on how we get success and more on the ends justifying any means. Is it any surprise that in business, sports and academia there is all manner of cheating that occurs?

Don't get me wrong. Goals are important. In a competition, you want to maintain a desire and a focus on winning. When I work with athletes our focus is on winning. When I help people create goals, I support them in shooting high, in succeeding; but not at any cost. Goals provide direction to life. Life, however, happens in the moments between our pursuits not just in the moments of accomplishment (or "not yet" accomplishments). Think about this. How long do you celebrate a success? Does that last anywhere near the amount of time you spent pursuing the goal? Or do you, more or less quickly, move on to the next pursuit? Or perhaps life will move you quickly to your next responsibility. Indeed, neurological research shows that positive experiences don't shape our brain unless we take time to really experience and absorb them.

The gold medal does not give you a life. Financial wealth does not give you a life. You can have a life with a gold medal and you can have a gold medal without a life. You can have financial wealth with a life and you can have financial wealth without a life. When my client and I explored how much time he took to even enjoy his accomplishments, he realized that in his 40 plus years he had spent very little time living and a lot of time pursuing. I applauded his tenacity at achieving his goals; but what is the point of success if not for life – for living. His life was happening in the moments between his achievements and his was missing out. Indeed, he was at risk of losing it all.

Pursuit of happiness and happiness are not the same thing. Back in the 1950s scientists discovered, quite by accident, an area of the rat's brain that when stimulated released dopamine. The rats would do anything to get that part of the brain stimulated and this led scientists to believe that they found the neurological basis of happiness and pleasure. It turns out, however, that it is not happiness that is activated but arousal. A feeling of alertness and attentiveness with a sense of anticipation of reward. The neurotransmitter dopamine is released when our brain recognizes an opportunity for a reward. The role of dopamine is to get the whole system to pay attention in order to increase our effort and our success. In fact, in brain scans scientists can see dopamine activates in anticipation of reward but is quiet when people get rewarded. Anything we think will make us feel good can trigger this system. Our brain then, can lead us into an endless cycle of chasing rewards with very little sense of satisfaction[9].

This discussion reminds me of a poem by 19th century Greek poet Cavafy.

---

[9] If you are stuck in a cycle of pursuit or find yourself giving in to immediate gratification at the expense of your long-term goals I suggest you read Dr. McGonigal's book "The Willpower Instinct" which explain why you can get stuck neurologically and what you can do about it.

ITHAKA – Cavafy

As you set out for Ithaka
hope your road is a long one,
full of adventure, full of discovery.
Laistrygonians, Cyclops,
angry Poseidon-don't be afraid of them:
you'll never find things like that on your way
as long as you keep your thoughts raised high,
as long as a rare excitement
stirs your spirit and your body.
Laistrygonians, Cyclops,
wild Poseidon-you won't encounter them
unless you bring them along inside your soul,
unless your soul sets them up in front of you.

Hope your road is a long one.
May there be many summer mornings when,
with what pleasure, what joy,
you enter harbors you're seeing for the first time;
may you stop at Phoenician trading stations
to buy fine things,
mother of pearl and coral, amber and ebony,
sensual perfume of every kind-
as many sensual perfumes as you can;
and may you visit many Egyptian cities
to learn and go on learning from their scholars.

Keep Ithaka always in your mind.
Arriving there is what you're destined for.
But don't hurry the journey at all.
Better if it lasts for years,
so you're old by the time you reach the island,
wealthy with all you've gained on the way,

not expecting Ithaka to make you rich.
Ithaka gave you the marvelous journey.
Without her you wouldn't have set out.
She has nothing left to give you now.
And if you find her poor, Ithaka won't have fooled you.
Wise as you will have become, so full of experience,
you'll have understood by then what these Ithakas mean.

One of the key messages of this poem is that your goals provide the reason for the journey but life occurs in the journey not in the destination.[10] A cliché to be sure but it is nevertheless true. This is why wise teachers from all cultures speak about learning to live in the present. One of the ways to live more in the present is to pay as much attention to *how* you want to live as you do *what* you want to achieve. This is not a new idea. As religious scholar Karen Armstrong has pointed out, wisdom traditions from western philosophy and theology to eastern traditions all speak of the importance of virtues or right conduct in creating a happy life. Virtues are also considered essential in creating happy lives in the science of positive psychology. Attending to our values helps us pay attention to the journey of life.

Although there are many ways to categorize our values, I often divide them into two types that I refer to as the "what" values and the "how" values. "What" values involve things we would like to see in the world or to accomplish. For example, we may value hard work or family or peace. ***"How" values*** on the other

---

[10] The poem also highlights how we project our own demons and obstacles along the path of our life. That was the topic of the previous chapter.

hand are the principle we hold for how we wish to treat ourselves and others.

Can you identify your "how" values? I have asked this question to thousands of people in different contexts (including prisons) and different countries. I typically get a standard and, dare I say universal, set of principles that all people tend to believe (except perhaps those high in psychopathy). I will bet that your list looks something like this:

- Respect
- Compassion
- Equality
- Fairness
- Patience
- Tolerance
- Loyalty
- Honesty
- Kindness

This is not an exhaustive list but it represents some of the most common set of values that I hear. I will then ask my clients or my audience two questions. First, how do you feel about yourself when you violate these values? When you act disrespectfully, dishonestly, unfairly and so on. Sure, some people say they feel some satisfaction initially, especially if they believe the other person deserved their derision, but more generally and over time they report that they mostly feel badly about themselves. Then I ask how people feel when they live up to their values. To this question the answer is universally that people feel good about themselves. What does it mean that you feel good about yourself when you live your values and badly when you violate them?

I suggest that this means we all have our own internal compass that guides us to experiencing a good life. You don't need a psychologist, a priest or a judge to tell you your values or that it is important to live up to them. Your own experience in life tells you that these values work because you feel better about your life when you live them and worse about your life when you violate them. Like a compass our values can guide us when we feel lost, confused or angry by telling us which choices will lead to actions that support our life. They can also be used to help keep us on track.

We don't have to worry about being perfect though. A metaphor I learned from one of Steven Covey's 7 habits books really makes this point well. Did you know that pilots have very exact flight plans for their journey? Did you know that they also tend to be off their flight path 90% of the time? This happens because of external factors such as weather changes, flocks of birds or other planes entering their flight path or internal factors such as pilot distraction. Nevertheless, they still get to their destinations relatively close to when they are supposed to. They do this by using their instruments and continually correcting their path. We too can get off course due to internal and external factors. The real problems in flight travel and life don't come from getting off course; they come from staying off course. So, use your compass and check to see if you are on course to a good life.

This, however, raises a question. If values are so important why do so many people violate them? Let's dig deeper to find the answer and a new understanding that will help us stick with our values. If we simplify life, then we have two choices in how we behave. We can choose to react to what others are doing (e.g., an eye for an eye) or we can respond according to our values - period, full stop, no exceptions. When I ask people which is the better choice I almost exclusively hear that responding according to our values is better than reacting to what others are doing.

So, once again, why do so many people violate their values if they serve to help us create a better life? When I explore this with my clients the most common factor identified is that they don't want to be taken advantage of by others. They don't want to be doormats or victims to other's disregard. I often hear people say if someone treats me disrespectfully and I don't react then I am letting them take advantage of me. Let's explore this more deeply to see if it is true.

Let us take a hypothetical example of a day in the life of Joe Reactor. Joe reacts to other people and circumstances by giving at least as good as he gets. Joe gets up in the morning and its raining even though the forecast called for sun and he happens to be working outdoors today. How do you think he reacts to that news? He then goes down to his kitchen to get his morning coffee and finds that his wife left the coffee machine unplugged so no fresh coffee is made. How does he react now? Then, she comes in the front door with a coffee and muffin from his favorite café. How is he doing now? Then as he leaves for work he gets cut off. What happens now? When he gets to work one of his colleagues shares some good news about a bonus they are all likely to get. What is going on with Joe now? Then he finds out that this co-worker missed something that means more work for Joe. So, where is Joe at now? What do you notice about Joe's mood, behaviour, and life as you imagine these scenarios? Is Joe protecting himself from being a doormat?

When Joe reacts, his life and mood become unpredictable to himself. His mood depends more on factors external to him rather than how he chooses to feel. In fact, to protect himself from being a victim he has chosen to be a victim. He is a victim because he allows people and factors external to him decide his mood and behaviour. Now this is easy in the short term because it doesn't take much cognitive effort to react. Someone swears you swear back; someone pushes you push back. Not much thought required. Additionally, you don't have to take any responsibility. The common excuse is, "I only did this because you did that." For example, I only yelled because you didn't plug in the coffee machine. In the long run, however you have given up control of your life and you let other people's choices and behaviours (or your perceptions of their behaviours) decide how your life is going to go.

What about choosing to live your values? First, if you read the definition of "how" values carefully you would have noticed that it involves not only how you treat others but also how you treat yourself. Therefore, allowing yourself to be continuously victimized is not consistent with living your values. You may also have noticed that I referred to this approach as responding instead of reacting. You see, the opposite of reacting is not being passive and doing nothing. The opposite of reacting is responding skilfully to the situation in front of you using your values. This is harder in the short-term. If someone is being disrespectful it takes more energy and skill to figure out how to respond in a way that remains respectful to both of you while being clear that the disrespectful behaviour is not acceptable. In the long term however, by investing in your values, you build confidence and healthier relationships. You begin to epitomize the concept of Strong-Back Open-Heart where you demonstrate strength in respecting your place in the world and openness in respecting other people's needs. In doing so you are less likely to be seen as a target or a challenge to others and more likely to be seen as someone who walks the journey of his or her life with confidence and skill. This invites support and help from others.

It turns out that success is not dependent on the selfish pursuit of our goals. Remember Adam Grant's research on successful givers? In his seminal book *Give and Take*, Grant emphasised how helping others and building connections serves our success. He highlighted how givers are values driven individuals who support others unconditionally. Successful givers also had boundaries (they could say no when it was necessary) and they focused on raising everyone up including themselves. They situate themselves within the circle of care and compassion not separate

> **TRY THIS: Leading with your Values**
>
> Identify your values and place the list where you can see it on a regular basis
>
> When you are stuck or uncertain ask whether the action you are considering is consistent with your values
>
> If yes proceed.
>
> If no stop and take a step back and open your mindset (see previous chapters).
>
> Reconnect with your values and identify an action consistent with your values.

from it. In this way, they built great relationships and supports that helped them succeed. Others also want them to succeed because they want everyone to succeed. Indeed, employees who provide social support at work are more likely to receive promotion compared to those who isolate.

It matters then, how you live the moments of your life. How you choose to treat others and yourself. The seventh choice for living well is to **live the moments of your life with integrity.**

CHAPTER 8

THE CONNECTION IMPERATIVE

"We cannot live only for ourselves. A thousand fibers connect us with our fellow men; and among those fibers, as sympathetic threads, our actions run as causes, and they come back to us as effects." Rev. Henry Melville

THE CONNECTION IMPERATIVE

Imagine spending one month pursuing pleasure. Does this sound like it would be amazing? Do you think "if only I had the luxury to pursue pleasure I would be happy all the time?" This was the homework for half of an undergraduate class that was taught by psychologist Martin Seligman. In his book, *Authentic Happiness*, Seligman refers to a simple experiment where he measured the happiness and life satisfaction of his students and then randomly divided the class into two groups. One half of the class was given the assignment to seek out pleasure for the next month. The rest of the class was given the task of being generous for the next month. He then tracked their level of happiness and life satisfaction. Can you guess what happened?

The results were fascinating. The group that focused on pleasure had an initial spike in their scores followed by a drop. The generosity group, on the other hand, had a slow increase that eventually surpassed the pleasure group and then persisted. In fact, Seligman reported that many of the students in the generosity group chose to continue doing their homework even after the month ended. Other more formal studies have confirmed these results. For example, one group of studies showed that giving money away makes us feel better than receiving money or even spending money on ourselves. Let's look at why generosity was so impactful while pleasure failed to produce lasting results.

It turns out that we are wired to habituate to most

things. Whatever pleasure we seek, we eventually get used to it and it has diminishing returns. This is a biological fact. Our neurons are geared to fire when we experience novelty but there is reduced excitation when there is nothing new. This is in part how addiction works. We chase more and more of that external stimulus to try and get that original pleasure. I am sure that you experienced this in your own life. That new car was your pride and joy when you first bought it and you washed it regularly. A few months later you may get a scratch and shrug your shoulders. The new smart phone is so exciting but six months later maybe the newest one would be better.

Why did the generosity group experience greater positive changes and sustained those changes? Engaging in, receiving and even observing generosity releases the neuropeptide oxytocin. Oxytocin is the "love" or "bonding" chemical. It is released during love making, breast feeding, group cooperation and any form of deep human connection. It is even released during stress, especially when we reach out for help or are provided help and support. Acts of generosity make us feel connected to others in deep and meaningful ways.

It is connection that promotes lasting happiness and well-being. Research on happiness consistently documents that human connection overwhelmingly determines the difference between higher and lower levels of happiness. Recently, a major global study by the World Health Organization (WHO) found that social support and generosity were among the most important factors in determining well-being. One of the conclusions of the report stated that individuals' "capacity to flourish are deeply influenced by their social surroundings, including the opportunity to form relationships and engage with those around them (family members, friends, colleagues)." Isolation and disconnection, on the other hand, is associated with psychological distress and mental illness.

I saw an example of this in my visits to Greece before and after the major economic recession of 2008. After Greece entered the European Economic Union in 2001, there was a period of tremendous prosperity and opportunity that many Greeks experienced. In one visit to Greece during the economic boom, I went with my wife and some close friends (two couples that were also our neighbours) who were excited to see Greece and connect with the local people and culture. As we were all sitting on my uncle's balcony in Athens with several of my extended family members, one of my cousins remarked at the close friendship I had with my neighbours and lamented that many people in Greece had lost that sense of community in their pursuit of wealth. He commented that people felt wealthier but they were more stressed and less happy.

This contrasts with a more recent visit to Greece. With the country in a dramatic economic recession, I noticed that despite the tragedy of the economic conditions and the political upheaval, people seemed more connected and engaged with each other. My cousins confirmed this assessment. They talked about the very real financial hardships and economic uncertainty as stressful and threatening but also the sense of renewed connection and community as a buffer. They were no longer alone. In fact, global research shows that in calamities people tend to get together, focusing more on the common good of their community rather than themselves and paradoxically often feel a greater sense of connection, meaning and psychological well-being.

Similarly, studies from around the world show that recovery from post traumatic stress is influenced by whether the person is situated in a community that allows for connections and communal healing instead of communities that promote isolation in healing. From his own observations of trauma recovery in different communities, anthropologist Brandon Kohrt concluded that Posttraumatic Stress Disorder (PTSD) might best be considered a disorder of recovery because the context of recovery determines whether people get PTSD, how severe it becomes and the speed of recovery. Similarly, one of the most significant factors in the success of any psychotherapy is the quality of connection between therapist and client. In other words, connections prevent and heal trauma whereas isolation makes it worse. From my observations as a psychologist I would say that this is true for most mental health challenges. As Sebastian Junger summarizes in his book *Tribe,* societies in which

---

TRY THIS: Create High Quality Connections

Research highlights 4 useful ideas for building high quality connections:

1. Respectful engagement: be present, attentive and affirming
2. Support what others are doing
3. Trust: believe that you can depend on others and show it
4. Play: allow time to goof off with no outcome in mind

a sense of community and equality exists mitigate the effects of trauma, despair and distress while promoting psychological well-being.

Unfortunately, the modern pursuit of individualism and materialism is alienating and associated with mental illness. Despite globalization, much of human society has shifted to a socially isolating life style that has dire consequences for our well-being and often associated with increases in depression disorders. According to the WHO, the most significant causes of unhappiness and disability involve clinical depression and anxiety. These issues currently affect about 10% of the world population and account for about 20% of all disability worldwide. WHO research also highlighted that individuals in wealthy countries and in countries where income disparity was greatest experienced higher rates of depression.

What makes this fact worse is that the income disparity is growing in two thirds of the world's countries. Furthermore, many politicians are playing on the fears that increased disparity is creating by promoting isolationism. Yet, depression is fundamentally a disorder of isolation and disconnection. Disconnection creates an "every person for themselves" mindset and promotes increased disparity. This can become a vicious circle.

The pursuit of individualism and materialism then, frequently leads to experiences of disconnection that fragments our lives into separate isolated pieces. Fragmentation is so pervasive that even how we receive information about the world these days is frequently fragmented. It comes in bits and bytes (or text and tweets) that are often without context, without history, without an understanding of our responsibilities or abilities to respond. These experiences of disconnection and fragmentation have reached the point of endangering the survival of all life-forms on the planet. Specifically, this has led to separating ourselves from nature (i.e., nature is a resource to be exploited) and our consequent attempts to control nature. Some of the negative implications of our actions towards nature are obvious (e.g., global warming). How we treat nature is not so different from how we treat each other. Violence, for example, is often justified by excluding, objectifying[11] and dehumanizing the other.

The human response to fragmentation is to shift into protection and survival mode. In survival mode, our mind-body system constricts and narrows, keeping us stuck in unhealthy patterns. Psychologist Stephen Gilligan has succinctly referred to this state as neuromuscular lock. When the body is locked or frozen, we will feel constriction in our breathing and tension in the muscles. The mind will also shift to a narrow, fixed state. In her research, Barbara Fredrickson described this as a narrowing of the thought-action repertoire. In other words, we have decreased capacity to think and respond to our circumstances. This diminished cognitive state can manifest as certainty (a firm conviction that there is only one way to see things).

---

[11] Objectifying involves seeing people as parts (fragments) not whole human beings. This is why common insults involve calling people by body parts (e.g., A**hole, C**t, Pr**ck). Calling people these names typically serves to justify treating them abusively.

Certainty makes us feel safer by reducing anxiety and it sounds like a good thing. But certainty can manifest as fundamentalism and righteousness. We shouldn't just worry about other people's fundamentalism because when we close our hearts and mind about a person or situation, we too become disconnected and can justify violating our values. Certainty is not confidence; it is ego in a state of fear. It involves the loss of perspectives and possibilities. Certainty works against growth and success because with certainty there is no more room for exploration.

Let's be clear though, it is not wealth that is the cause of emotional distress. The WHO report also points out that wealth can promote well-being. Similarly, Martin Seligman points out that pleasure can be useful for our mental health – but only if we think of it as the dessert of life instead of the main course. The issue, as I see it, is whether we pursue wealth and pleasure in the context of our complete humanity or whether we pursue these at the expense of our humanity.

As you can see from the information presented, we are not just wired to seek rewards and survive; we are also wired to connect. So much so that not only does connection feel good and buffer us from hardship but people will even risk their lives for total strangers. Indeed, human beings first response to both threat and growth opportunities is social engagement; reaching out to connect with others. It is only when this fails because of isolation, neglect or abuse that we revert to survival patterns. We ignore this truth at our peril.

In summary, the emphasis on individualism and the pursuit of material needs and desires creates experiences of fragmentation and disconnection. Experiences of fragmentation and disconnection lead to neuromuscular lock. Neuromuscular lock works against change, growth, flexibility and adaptability by creating closed biological and psychological systems. Outwardly, neuromuscular lock manifests as fear and certainty which promotes a fixed rather than growth mindset both in individuals and in society.

The antidote to fragmentation is connection. The pathway to connection is compassion. In states of compassion we step outside of ourselves and connect with others. We also have a desire to engage in the world to address the suffering we see or to promote life affirming change. Compassion then connects us to the realities of the material world but in a way in which we are also connected to the experiences of others.

What is compassion? How do we understand it? When I ask people to share the images they have of compassion, they tend to report very stereotypical soft gentle expressions of, for example, holding another in suffering. Similarly, in a google images search of the word compassion I noted three dominant categories of images (see Figure 1). First, are images that include hearts. Second, are the prototypical images of gentleness and care. Finally, there are the utopian images such as the biblical lion and the lamb lying together or a popular one sent to me once that had a lion and a zebra hugging out their differences.

Figure 1

There is nothing inherently wrong with these images or the understandings they represent except that they are too narrow. This soft, utopian, narrow representation can lead to compassion fatigue and compassion anxiety. For example, people begin to wonder if being compassionate and forgiving would lead to becoming victimized? (What if the lion changes its mind?) People also question whether opening to the suffering of others would overwhelm them and leave them collapsing into grief, helplessness and despair? This often leads to seeing compassion as a weakness in a "survival of the fittest" world. As such compassion is seen as an experience that needs to be avoided when possible and activated only for those few deserving people (usually those with whom we most identify).

Compassion however, is larger than these images represent. Compassion can also be *sharp* as in the surgeon using a scalpel to remove a tumor; it can *strong* as in the case of individuals involved in nonviolent resistance movements; and it can be tremendously *courageous* as is demonstrated by the individuals involved in restorative justice and healing circles. I refer to this as *Intelligent Compassion* to distinguish it from the simplified view described earlier. Intelligent compassion involves connection and caring. It involves a desire to promote life affirming change. Intelligent Compassion also has boundaries and involves skillfulness. By skillfulness I mean the capacity to do the right thing at the right time by being in the right state. In this way, it is differentiated from unidimensional understandings of compassion as simply a "soft" sympathetic emotion and from "tough love" ideas that are blunt instruments often used for control and masquerading as compassion.

When I told Bill (from chapter three) that he needed an emotional enema and ended the session, it wasn't tough love. I wasn't trying to teach him a lesson. I was genuinely worried about his welfare and I knew that I could not help him in that state. The comment was not planned. It arose out of concern and a need to decline his invitations to support his unhealthy focus while inviting him to take responsibility.

Furthermore, Bill new I wasn't being cruel or coercive. Authenticity matters with compassion. As Daniel Siegel, a pioneer in the field of interpersonal neurobiology has suggested, human beings have a sort of neural Wi-Fi in which we are connected at a subconscious level. Evidence of this can be found in the fields of neurology and neuro-cardiology. One example involves mirror neurons which activate in the premotor cortex to reflect and decode facial expressions and thus the emotional state of the person being observed. According to Jeffery Schwartz of the UCLA Neuropsychiatric Institute, this decoding happens primarily in a right brain to right brain process that is often below conscious awareness but is nevertheless felt by the observer. Thus, you can't pretend compassion when you have contempt. The contempt will leak out and be felt, changing the context of the interaction.

> **TRY THIS: Seeing the basic human goodness of others**
> (Kornfield, 2008)
>
> - Begin with the premise that all people have a basic human goodness and nobility of spirit and that we are all connected at this level of our full humanity.
> - Start during a day when you are in a good mood.
> - Set a clear intention that during the day you will look for the inner nobility and goodness of three people.
> - Notice how this perception affects: your interactions with them; your own experience of yourself; your behaviour. (Write/journal this experience)
> - Do this 5 more times (save more difficult people for later)
> - Next choose one day per week to do this consistently for one to two months
> - When you are ready expand to more days; do it on more stressful days; and/or do it with people you find difficult.

Intelligent compassion is both a felt experience that can be cultivated and an engagement skill that can be learned. Neurological research highlights that compassion is an emotional competency that improves with practice. The more you practice compassion, the more you feel it and the more your brain changes to support you making the choices that lead to living well.

Compassion regulates physiology such that it increases connection to our own higher brain functions thus promoting wisdom and creativity. In states of compassion we see more broadly and can respond more effectively rather than react to the immediate circumstance in a narrow-prescribed way.

Compassion also promotes accountability. In states of compassion we recognize that it is only in responsibility that change is possible. Additionally, self-compassion tends to activate the neurological resources that help individuals make better choices whereas being tough on oneself tends to activate the stress response system and facilitates reacting with the same old bad habits.

Intelligent compassion also facilitates success in life. Recall that givers represent the top performers across a wide variety of professions and careers. Successful givers are compassionate, generous, with strong values and clear, flexible and healthy boundaries. They are also interested in everyone's success (including their own). Because of this attitude and approach, Adam Grant noted that successful givers developed extensive positive relationships and connections that also facilitated their success. Successful givers are exquisite examples of individuals demonstrating intelligent compassion.

Living with compassion and integrity does not prevent tragedy from occurring in your life. It does, however, help you build resiliency and the personal and communal resources to navigate these challenges. So why not cultivate intelligent compassion? One way to do this is to try the generosity experiment yourself for one month and see how it goes. I know what your thinking. I don't have the time or money to be generous everyday for a month. Keep in mind that generosity does not need to "cost" you anything. You can be generous with your smiles, with kind words, with letting people ahead of you in a line. Remember too, that the research shows that generosity pays dividends in your own well-being so the investment is well worth it. Again, don't take my word for it. Try it for a month. One final piece of advice though. Don't just "do" generosity as a check list item that needs to be completed in your to do list. When you act generously, allow yourself to connect with the act and the receiver even for just ten seconds.

> **TRY THIS: Personal Generosity Experiment**
>
> Identify the different ways you can be generous.
>
> Do not give so much that you cannot meet your own needs.
>
> For four weeks, engage in one act of generosity each day.
>
> Make sure to be generous with strangers as well as family and friends.

You can also cultivate intelligent compassion by engaging in compassion based practices. Try the "seeing the basic goodness of others" exercise from page 98 as a start and refer to chapter nine for more exercises. Remember, for a healthy and successful life **demonstrate intelligent compassion and choose to build community and connections.**

EIGHT CHOICES: Summary

Choice 1:
Focus on where you want to go and what you want to create.

Choice 2:
Consume information consciously and absorb life affirming information

Choice 3:
Take responsibility for your action

Choice 4:
Balance your energy on a regular basis

Choice 5:
Reframe problems into opportunities

Choice 6:
Open your mindset to possibilities

Choice 7:
Live the moments of your life with integrity

Choice 8:
Build community and connections through intelligent compassion

In the introduction, I noted that the eight choices revolve around two key themes: attention and intelligent compassion. In these eight chapters, we identified that attention is critical because whatever we focus on will expand in or consciousness and, moreover, we will move towards the object of our focus. Without training our attention, we are at the mercy of what pulls our attention. This often leads to focusing on the obstacles of life and being pulled into negative messages and limiting beliefs that shrink our life. Our mind and body constrict, creating further limits on what we see is possible. When we get stuck in negative beliefs we often also give up responsibility for our life. This seems easy at first because it takes energy to be responsible, but then we notice that we have also given up our freedom.

We can, however, re-orient our attention by taking responsibility and opening ourselves up. We learned that intelligent compassion helps open our mind and body to possibility taking us out of neuromuscular lock. Compassion furthermore allows us to release the objects of our attention that keep us stuck (e.g., past resentments) and increases a sense of empowerment and accountability for our lives. Through living with intelligent compassion, we build healthy relationships with others and ourselves that support our life. Finally, through intelligent compassion we understand when we need to open and when we need to solidify our boundaries so that we can adjust to each situation in a way that promotes life affirming action for ourselves and others.

In some ways, these eight choices are very simple decisions we can make that will allow us to build an exceptional and fulfilling life while overcoming the challenges we will inevitably face. Simple does not mean easy. Effort and commitment is required. Initially it may feel difficult to expend the energy but over time these choices become habits that we can move towards more and more easily. This brings us to chapter nine which provides a framework and a set of practices that can help us integrate these choices in our life more easily.

CHAPTER 9

CORE:
PRACTICES & EXERCISES

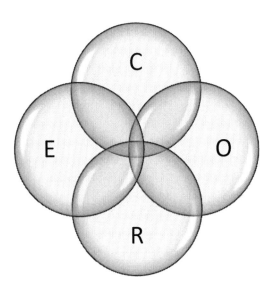

"A strong core will improve your technique, strength, and stamina and compliment everything you do." Susan Trainor

CORE:

Practices & Exercises

I hope that in the preceding chapters you gained knowledge that will be useful to you in building a healthy and satisfying life. Knowledge alone, however, rarely leads to change. Knowledge must be mobilized into action. In this chapter, I will introduce you to several exercises and practices that, if applied, will help you move that knowledge into life affirming action so that you can make the choices that promote your health, success and well-being.

I refer to the exercises in this chapter as CORE practices for several reasons. In physical health, exercise specialists frequently refer to the need to work out our core (the muscles around our trunk and pelvis). Core strength creates physical stability and balance that supports all our physical activities. Similarly, the exercises discussed in this chapter focus on our psychological core and practicing them creates psychological stability and balance that supports our life. CORE is also an acronym that simplifies and identifies the four complementary sets of practices that create psychological stability and balance. Specifically, CORE stands for Centering, Opening, Releasing and Extending. Finally, the word core also means fundamental or essential and these practices are, in my opinion, fundamental for success.

Let's describe each of these four essential sets of practices. When I was involved in Aikido training I heard several ideas that stuck with me not only as essential for martial arts training but also for life training. One such saying was "first center then extend into the field." If you are not centered in an aikido competition, you will get knocked down quickly. Similarly, if you are not centered in life you collapse quickly in the face of any challenge. The first set of practices discussed in this chapter therefore involve exercises in centering and grounding ourselves.

The second set of practices can also be illuminated by another expression I heard associated with Aikido. A teacher of mine, psychologist Stephen Gilligan, who was also a student of Aikido, once stated that it was important "not to give your eyes away." In Aikido, training includes learning how to have "soft eyes" that are not fixated on one thing. My interpretation of these expressions is that if we fixate on the challenge (or challenger) we get stuck in reacting rather than responding. Instead, if we open to the whole field we can see the challenge but also the many ways we can move to respond to what is in front of us. The second set of practices therefore involve learning to create open states for creativity and adaptation.

The third set of practices involve reclaiming wasted energy. Frequently in therapy I hear people talk about how they wished things could have been different or they speak of historic slights and resentments. I typically ask these clients, tongue in cheek, where they have their time machine stored. You see most people spend a tremendous amount of energy focusing on things that they cannot change, especially from their past. Learning how to wisely release energy that is being siphoned to the impossible task of changing the past can be tremendously helpful in shifting our focus back to health and life. The third set of practices then involves exercises in releasing or letting go of what is holding us back.

For the last set of practices, we can go back to that initial expression I mentioned. The latter part of the "center then extend" idea is that we must inevitably move into the field. This is where the action exists; where life exists. The last set of practices then, involve attending to and energizing what we wish to create in our lives. Creating a life takes more than belief and faith, it requires taking affirmative action even without guarantees of success. We will therefore explore strategies that will help us extend into the field of life in ways that promote well-being and success.

These four sets of practices are not linear. They are not simply 4 steps we engage in one after the other. Instead, they are complementary and interactive practices that we move in and through at various times as we work on creating balance, stability and energy for the life we are creating (See figure 2). As I was reviewing the resources I used for helping people in these areas I realized that there was a separate book worth of material available and I could not include it all in this chapter. What I have done is provided you with enough practices in this chapter to get you started. I have also pointed you to resources where you can access additional practices.

Figure 2: CORE Practices

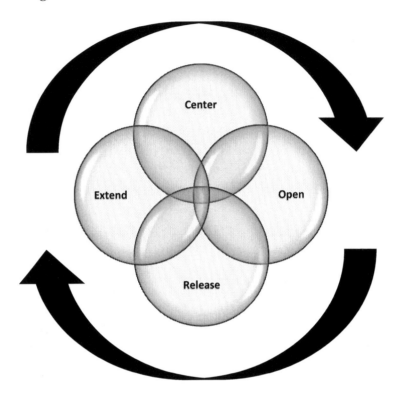

Center

Attention acts like a filter directing our resources to one thing and away from something else. The more intense our focus the more powerful the effect. Understanding how to use attention is therefore central to steering our minds to where we want to go in life and consuming information that supports us while spitting out what doesn't nourish us. This involves strengthening and cleansing our minds on a regular basis so that we have the mental resources to cultivate awareness and discernment. What are broadly called self-regulation or grounding exercises are essential for this task. These include breathing exercises and meditation. These exercises center us so that we can move through life with more stability.

I sometimes refer to these practices as mental hygiene. Mental hygiene is just as important as, for example, dental hygiene. Think about how often you brush your teeth each day. Most people brush their teeth twice a day without fail. Even when they are stressed out and busy. We rarely, if ever, say I don't have time to brush my teeth. We just do it. Why? Because it has become a healthy habit that we don't question and because we don't want the consequences of bad breath and cavities. We brush our teeth even if we only consume healthy food.

The same is true for the mind as it is with our teeth. The bad breath of the mind are the things we say that we regret and that turn people off. The cavities of the mind are the negative beliefs, attitudes and habits that keep us trapped in a less fulfilling life. And just like brushing our teeth we need to practice cleansing and strengthening our mind regularly even if we have only consumed healthy information (which is unlikely). Indeed, why would we expect our mind to stay strong and healthy if we never clean and exercise it?

Indeed, grounding has been shown to have positive effects on us physically (e.g., reducing inflammation), emotionally (e.g., improving mood) and cognitively (e.g., improving concentration). Furthermore, research shows that when we use these exercises on a regular basis our brains change to support us. By practicing the various mental hygiene exercises, we strengthen the prefrontal cortex increasing our capacity to stay present, aware and responsive (instead of reactive) to our environments.

> **TRY THIS: Basic Self-Regulation Exercise:**
>
> Breath in for 5 seconds (pause 1 sec)
>
> Breath out for 5 seconds (pause 1 sec).
>
> Do this 10-12 times per day for 5 breaths each time.

One of the first exercises I give all my clients involves a practice of slowing down their breathing. Slowing down breathing to 4-6 breaths per minute increases our heart rate variability which is associated with an activation of the prefrontal cortex and a deactivation of the stress response system. Given that we are constantly bombarded with negative, fear based information I recommend that my clients download an application on their smart phones that will signal them at random intervals to stop and breathe in this way. By doing this regularly for just one minute at a time, they can tone down the stress response system throughout the day. Alternatives to using an application on the phone would involve using cues in the environment. For example, with clients who have driving anxiety I often recommend that they take at least one breath this way every stop sign and every red light. You can use other environmental cues including objects, colours or repetitive behavioural patterns (e.g., every time you drink water or coffee) to signal that it is time to take five breaths in this way. It only takes one minute. Why not give it a try?

You can also get grounded by finding your physical center. I often ask clients whose bodies are expressing collapse (e.g., shoulders slumped) to sit tall

---

TRY THIS: Physical Grounding

Use your Senses:

Name 5 things you hear, see, and feel through the body. Pick some scents and take a moment to pay attention to the aromas. Find something to eat and take your time, notice all aspects of the experience and chew slowly noting all the tastes.

Take off your shoes and socks and walk on the ground. Place your attention on the soles of your feet. Feel the earth supporting you.

Sit tall on your sit bones. With your eyes closed, find your center by making micro-movements until you feel the center. Notice what changes when you are centered.

Imagine:

Sit or stand straight with your feet firmly on the ground. Imagine that you are a mighty tree and sense your roots penetrating the earth deep and wide supporting your growth. Dig deep so that you can also reach high.

in their chair and find their sit bones. The sit bones are quite literally the bones under the flesh of your bottom that you sit on. I then ask them to close their eyes and find the position in which they feel perfectly centered. You can do this by making micro movements forward, back and side to side until you feel the center point. From this centered position, I often ask them to attend to the issue that was causing them to feel collapse and notice what changes have occurred in their attitude, perspective and sense of what they can do to address this issue. Typically, people's perspective expands, their attitude improves and they see new options for responding to their circumstances. This is because our body effects our mind as much as our mind effects our body.

Additionally, grounding involves connecting more strongly to the body and to the physical reality around you. There are a variety of ways to engage in physical grounding. For example, you can connect with your senses. Paying close attention and naming what you see, hear, sense (kinaesthetically), smell and taste[12] can be a powerful grounding exercise. Helping people ground in their current sensory experience is one way to stop panic episodes[13]. Another simple exercise is to walk barefoot in nature, on grass or sand

---

[12] Remember the eating raisins exercise described in the beginning of the book.

[13] Panic episodes typically involve people having catastrophic thinking that activates the stress response system and then creates physiological changes that are interpreted as life threatening. For example, the constriction of the pectoral muscles is interpreted as a heart attack. This creates further catastrophic thoughts and physiological activation. Grounding in present moment sensory experience stops the cascade of catastrophic thinking and thereby turns off the stress response system and the physiological symptoms.

for example, and really feel your feet connected to the earth. Using your imagination also works. You can, for example, imagine yourself rooting like a tree into the earth. This activates a felt sense experience of grounding.

Remember also that a repetition of words can create a shift in our mind-body states. In my training, I learned three simple words that can act as focal points to create a centered experience in practitioners. These words are Silence, Stillness and Spaciousness. Repeating these words helps quiet the mind, relax the body and open the mind-body state to possibility. Adding imagery to the words can also amplify the effect. For example, with silence imagining the quiet of night, with stillness imagining the solidness of a mountain and with spaciousness an open field.

Finally, I always teach my clients how to use mindfulness meditation. There are various ways in which one can do mindfulness practices but they all share the following features: present centered attention and acceptance of experience (nonjudgmental attitude). Below you will find a description of two common exercise I teach my clients (see pages 115 & 116). One version uses cognitive anchor points (adapted from a version that Thich Nhat Han teaches) and the other uses the breath and the body as the anchor point. Some people prefer one over the other so use the version that works best for you. If the words used in the cognitive anchor exercise don't suit you, you can use either the repetition of a mantra (any words you choose to repeat), the centering prayer or simply count your breaths on prayer beads. A variety of guided exercises can be found on the internet and on my website: www.drharry.ca/products.

Research has shown that after two months of daily mindfulness practice, changes can be documented in the brain. These changes include an increase in metabolic activity and grey matter in the frontal cortex. What transforms, however, is not the nature of your thoughts but your relationship to your thoughts. Let me explain what I mean. It turns out we have a lot of thoughts per day. Some estimates put the number between 50,000 and 80,000[14]. From your own experience, you know that some of those thoughts are brilliant and some are stupid, some are beautiful thoughts and others are ugly thoughts, some are sane thoughts while other thoughts are downright crazy. It's the nature of the mind to travel the gamut of possible thoughts. It's what allows for creativity. Many people, however, are caught up repeating the same thoughts over and over having created a habit of thinking that is then reinforced by neural pathways. When we engage in mental hygiene practices we don't stop negative thoughts from occurring. What changes is that these no longer trigger a cascade of associated negative thinking patterns. We simply notice and release thoughts that don't serve us.

Mindfulness is useful for centering, opening and releasing. We center by anchoring into present moment experiences. Doing so also opens us up, over

---

[14] This range is often mentioned by both professionals and other writers. The National Science Foundation, however, estimated 50,000 thoughts per day as most accurate. All estimates are controversial because, let's face it, this is difficult to measure. Nevertheless, we can, just by paying attention to our experience, appreciate that we have a lot of thoughts every day.

> **TRY THIS: Mental Hygiene - Mindfulness with Cognitive Anchor**
>
> Start by sitting tall (with a strong back and open heart)
>
> Name your intention to stay present for the next few minutes.
>
> Noticing your breathing. Noticing the breath in and out.
>
> For 1 minute say, "Breathing In" as you breathe in and "Breathing Out" as you breathe out.
>
> For 1 minute say, "Deep" as you breathe in and "Slow" as you breathe out.
>
> For 1 minute say, "Calm" as you breathe in and "Relaxed" as you breathe out.
>
> For 1 minute say, "Present Moment" as you breathe in and "Wonderful Moment" as you breathe out.
>
> For 1 minute say and experience, "Smile" as you breathe in and "Peace" as you breathe out.

time, to seeing the fullness of experience in the moment without judgment. This helps us see more clearly as we choose to move forward. Finally, the training also involves practicing letting go of distraction. By repeatedly noticing when we are thinking (instead of focusing on the anchor point), labelling the experience and then returning to the anchor we gain essential practice in letting go. Mindfulness then is, in my opinion, one of the most fundamental practices we can engage in to help ourselves enter states that allow us to more effectively create the life we desire.

> **TRY THIS: Mental Hygiene - Mindfulness with Somatic Anchor**
>
> Start by sitting tall (with a strong back and open heart)
>
> Name your intention to stay present for the next few minutes.
>
> Close eyes and start by focusing in on your breathing. If your mind wonders away while we do the exercise simply say "thinking" to yourself and return to the process without judging yourself or the thoughts. (about 30 seconds)
>
> As you breathe out drop your attention to your feet. Notice the sensation and energy in your feet at this moment. Notice that your feet are connected to the ground. Feel the sensation in the bottom of your feet as you breathe out. (about 1 minute)
>
> With your next breath in bring your attention to your knees. As you breath in focus on the sensations, perceptions ad subtle energetic feeling in your knees at this moment….then as you breath out drop your attention to your feet…. Breathing in attention is on your knees…breathing out your attention is on your feet. (about 1 minute)
>
> With your next breath in bring your attention to your hands…as you breathe in notice the weight of your hands…the temperatures of your hands…the subtle energetic aliveness of your own hands. ….then as you breathe out drop your attention to your feet…. Breathing in to your hands…breathing out your attention is on your feet. (about 1 minute)
>
> With your next breath in bring your attention to the crown of your head…to the very top of your head…so with each breath in your focusing on the sensations, perceptions and the subtle energetic feelings on the crown of your head at this moment…whatever they may be… then as you breathe out drop your attention to your feet…breathing in to the crown…breathing out to the feet…take ten full breathes this way (about…1.5minutes)

Open

Opening expands our capacity so that we can see beyond our challenges and even beyond our goals. When we open we enter a larger creative space by seeing life more broadly. We can see the forest as well as the trees. Opening involves being able to get outside our belief boxes and shifting to positive emotional states so that we can access our own wisdom and intelligence.

As discussed in the previous chapter, we can open through acts of generosity. Generosity activates oxytocin and shifts our neurological activity. It also builds connections thereby adding additional resources. A simple rule for generosity is the 5-minute favor discussed in Adam Grant's book. Simply put you should be willing to help anyone when their request would take 5 minutes or less. I frequently take the time responding to individuals for whom I cannot offer services by connecting them with someone who can help them. I have heard that this, in part, helped create my reputation as someone who genuinely cares about the welfare of people. As you can imagine, a reputation of caring increases credibility in my profession.

> **TRY THIS: Five Minute Favor**
>
> Follow through with any request that takes 5 minutes or less to fulfill

In addition to practicing generosity, we can also open by practicing gratitude. When we activate a feeling of gratitude, we increase our heart rate variability, thereby calming down our nervous system and opening our cognitive resources. Researchers at the Heart Math Institute point out that in doing so we also activate the intelligence of the heart which has its own neural network. This creates heart-brain entrainment in which the combined intelligence or wisdom is greater than the sum of its parts.

Gratitude is simple to practice. You can start a gratitude journal as many authors have recommended. You can also take a few moments every day and just attend to something (or someone) for which you are grateful. A one-minute focus on gratitude can be enough to create a shift. With practice, you can activate a state of gratitude at any time.

> **TRY THIS: Gratitude Exercise**
>
> Shift attention to your heart
>
> Call up a feeling of gratitude for anything or anyone in your life
>
> Notice the feelings and sensation that are associated with the feeling of gratitude
>
> Breathe these feeling in and through your heart in whatever way makes sense to you. Let the feeling spread throughout your body
>
> You can do short bursts of gratitude for 30 seconds several times a day and/or you can do this for longer periods of time (say 5 minutes)

It is important to understand, however, that to achieve the shift in state you cannot simply think about what you are grateful for; you must also feel it. It must be a full mind-body experience. The object of the gratitude is less important than the feeling activated. You do not have to be grateful for something large; it can be as simple as a good cup of coffee. It is the quality of the feeling that counts.

We can also practice the Aikido technique of soft eyes. The practice involves relaxing the muscles around our eyes and letting ourselves see with our peripheral vision as well as with our central, focused vision. It is a form of three-pointed attention practice. Your simultaneously attend, for example, to the walls on either side of you as well as the wall in front of you, thereby opening your gaze. You can also place your hands on your knees while sitting and add an object in front of you. Practice attending to all three areas at the same time. Remember this is called soft eyes. It is a gentle practice so let go of any tension as you do this. Don't force it. The goal is to take in the whole field without being distracted or fixated on any one thing. In this way, the brain learns to become more open to the diversity of possibilities that surround us.

Openness also occurs best in the context of others and in feeling connected. You never know what opportunities will be presented and from what direction they will arise. In his writing, Shawn Achor discusses how collective intelligence increases when we can share our positive reality with others and thereby increasing our own capacity and success. Stephen Gilligan refers to something similar in his discussion of "generative intelligence." Generative intelligence describes the experience in which the collective sum of resources and capacity that occurs when people connect or feel connected is greater than the sum of their parts. Through connections we open to resources larger than just our own.

> **TRY THIS: Soft Eyes Practice**
>
> Sit with a strong back and an open heart
>
> Pick three points of attention. One on either side of you and one in front of you.
>
> Soften your eyes and open your gaze so that you attend to all three points.
>
> Stay open to the three points and the whole field.
>
> Release any distraction or fixation that occurs and soften eyes again.

Another way to feel connection and open yourself is to practice compassion. Compassion based practices have been shown to shift neurological activity away from the parts of the brain that focus on the self and increase neural activity in parts involved in understanding others and regulating emotions. For example, researchers have found that practicing loving-kindness meditation increased activity in the inferior parietal cortex which associated with empathy. Concurrently, there was an increase in the dorsolateral prefrontal cortex which is involved in positive emotions and regulating emotionally difficult experiences. Noted psychiatrist Dan Seigel has concluded that compassion helps promote brain integration increasing our internal resources and our capacity to live effectively in the world.

TRY THIS: Compassion Meditation Practice

1. Take your awareness in your heart, sensing what emotions are present

2. Cultivating love and appreciation for yourself (Repeat: *"may I be well, may I be happy, may I be free of suffering"*)

3. Suffering person: for example, compassion for the victim(s) of abuse (Repeat: *"may they be well, may they be happy, may they be free of suffering"*)

4. Neutral person: someone you do not know (e.g., an ordinary Afghani who is experiencing fear and deprivation due to conflict) (Repeat: *"may they be well, may they be happy, may they be free of suffering"*)

5. Difficult person: call to mind a person you are having difficulty with or a group in general. We may despise the actions that they have committed. Yet we can still recognize that this person (or persons) suffers. Their frustration and anger and their fear are painful to them, and are the cause of pain for others. We can wish this person well, wishing that the hatred in his or her heart be healed by love. (Repeat: *"May they be well, may they be happy, may they be free from suffering".*)

6. All sentient beings (Repeat: *"May all sentient beings be well, may all sentient beings be happy, may all sentient beings be free from suffering".*)

7. *Let go of act of wishing others well – Relax back into awareness of yourself.*

8. *Spend a few minutes absorbing the practice*

- *Note: Be gentle and persistent: bringing your awareness back to your heart with patience and kindness.*

We can also open by cultivating curiosity. Think about the boundless curiosity of children that manifests in the form of endless questions. One study suggests that four-year-old children ask a question about every 2 minutes. Questions are essential for learning and development.

In his examination of innovation, journalist Warren Berger concluded that the skill of asking questions is essential for creativity and a catalyst for innovative change. In his book, *A More Beautiful Question*, he argues that innovators focus on questions that can be acted upon. This contrasts with what I refer to as quicksand or blackhole questions that keep you stuck. As noted in chapter one, questions that focus on changing the past are not useful. Nor are questions that make us feel powerless (e.g., why did this happen to me?).

> **TRY THIS:**
>
> **Beautiful Questions**
>
> OPEN:
>
> - Brainstorm only with questions
> - **Why** questions: Why does a particular situation exist? Why has no one addressed this? Why do I want to invest time on this?
>
> EXPLORE POSSIBILITIES:
>
> - **What if** questions: what if we focused on what is working? What if I saw this issue from a new perspective?
>
> ACTION ORIENTATION
>
> - **How** questions: How do I make this happen? How do I test this idea? How do I keep motivated?
> - **Who** will support me?
> - **Who** has knowledge that would be helpful?

Beautiful questions, on the other hand, open our focus and invite us to search for new possibilities and inspire action (e.g., "why does it have to be this way?" "How can it be different?"). Berger describes numerous innovators and change makers who made an impact by starting with a question. For example, he describes how Reed Hastings started Netflix by first asking, "Why should I pay these late fees?' and then, "What if video rental was run like a health club?"

Berger emphasises the why, what if and how questions. I would like to suggest that the who question is equally important. First, in terms of, "If not you than whom?" In other words, you too can take responsibility to make this change/innovation happen. Who, is also important in activating the collective intelligence and in recognition that success does not occur in isolation but through support and community. Who is your community of care and support? Who can you connect with to find the resources and guidance you will need?

Lastly, I will remind you again of the suggestions made in the previous chapters. Opening is facilitated by training our capacity to see multiple view points. Take some time each week to practice increasing your perspectives. Shawn Achor has suggested another practice that is useful. He asks people to pick any task and identify both positive and negative aspects to the experience. The task can be as simple as washing the dishes. For example, negative aspects of washing dishes might be: it's boring; I could be doing something more productive, and so on. Positive aspects can include: there is a sense of accomplishment, I am promoting the health of all family members by keeping things clean; I can listen to my favorite music while I wash, and so on. Practice with different tasks. Can you think of positive views of these task as well as negative views? Can you get 3 positives to every negative aspect?

Release

Earlier I discussed how mental hygiene doesn't prevent negative thinking but it changes our relationship to negative thoughts such that we can release and refocus to more effective understandings and actions. Anthony De Mello, a psychologist and Jesuit monk, expressed this well in one of his lectures. He noted that before he became awake and aware to his life, he was depressed. He then remarked that after he woke up he was still depressed but it didn't bother him anymore. He had cultivated a different relationship to his thoughts and moods such that he could notice them without being attached to them. In this way, the thoughts and moods did not get stuck.

I had a direct experience of this after I finally chose to practice meditation regularly. For years, I dabbled with meditation but never turned it into a habit or lifestyle. When I finally did, I noticed a change in how I related to life and to my own thinking. The changes were subtle and at first, I did not necessarily notice anything significant expect that I usually felt more relaxed after practicing. I finally noticed how meditation effected my life when my car got broke into.

To help you understand why this was a different experience I need to take you back to my early twenties. I considered myself a good guy who tried to stay respectful but I could also be volatile and reactive. I remember this one day when I went to get my car from a parking lot and it was missing. I went ballistic. Initially I thought that my car was stolen. I did eventually realize that it was likely towed as I had over stayed my welcome in this parking lot but I was still furious. I yelled and screamed (at no one in particular) and threw my nap sack across the parking lot. I basically had an adult tantrum. Of course, it did nothing to change my situation. My day was ruined and I ruminated about this over and over again for days effecting my life negatively again and again.

Ten years later, and after practicing meditation daily for over six months, I was going to the parking lot to get my car and it was missing. I immediately experienced negative thoughts arise in my mind as well as revenge fantasies for the individual or individuals who stole my car (this was my residential parking so I was certain it was stolen and not towed this time). But as these thoughts arose, I noticed them, but I was not attached to them. There was this distance where I could see the thoughts would not be helpful. I took a breath and decided to walk up to the entrance to see if the thieves were able to get out. It turns out they abandoned my car at the gate as they could not leave without a remote. My guess is they waited for some time for someone to be coming home so they could get out but after a while they got bored and just abandoned the vehicle. I walked to my car. There was no damage. They were that good at breaking in and ironically that was good news for me as I did not have any repairs to make. So, I got in my car and drove to work. That was it. No carrying the incident through my day or letting it ruin my mood. I did, however, get an immobilization device.

That evening when I reflected on the event, I noticed that I responded to this situation whereas in the past I had reacted. I realized that this difference was crucial. The same negative thoughts and feelings can arise (and did arise) but I had cultivated a different relationship to my thoughts and emotions. My ability to respond to the circumstances in my life, even the negative circumstances, had changed for the better.

The other thing I want you to understand is that I did not suppress the negative thoughts and feelings. I just didn't indulge in them. Suppressing thoughts and feelings doesn't work (remember the pink elephants). There is an adage that says what we resist will persist. Some people suggest that this explains why dieting does not work. When you diet, you are trying to supress desires for some foods which then activates a focus on that which you are trying to supress.

> **TRY THIS: Letting Go Exercise**
>
> 1. Center yourself. Breathing in raise your awareness to your forehead. Breathing out focus on your feet and the ground.
> 2. As you breathe in notice the thoughts and feelings that you experience as negative. Name them. Acknowledge that they are difficult and that you are not alone in having these kinds of experiences.
> 3. Breathing out allow the thoughts and feelings to follow your breath and attention to your feet and the ground. Release them into the earth saying gently "I let this go."
> 4. Repeat. Be patient with the process.

Rather than trying to supress these thoughts, it is much more effective to accept the thoughts without trying to push them away or indulge in them. To make peace with negative thoughts simply accept that it's the nature of the mind to experience the gamut of possible thinking so you give yourself permission to think and feel whatever occurs without having to believe that what arises must be true or needs to be followed. Indeed, research by neuroscientist Phillip Goldin reveals that when people accept rather than supress negative thoughts and feelings, the stress response decreased in these individuals.

Mindfulness helps accomplish this however there are other practices that may be helpful. Another way I have been teaching clients how to let go is to focus on the negative thoughts and feelings as they breathe in and to allow the thought and feeling to dissolve as they breathe out. I have a more in-depth exercise in my website called *compassionate letting go* that is especially useful for strong feelings where the simpler exercise does not suffice. As with all these exercises it is important to remember that change is not instantaneous but rather occurs through repetition and practice.

We can also practice releasing negative thoughts and beliefs through cognitive restructuring exercises. There are many ways to do this and psychologists skilled in Cognitive-Behavioural Therapy can help you. Socratic questions are one way to use cognitive restructuring to challenge negative thoughts and beliefs. Socrates was an early proponent of using beautiful questions to open minds and create positive change.

The purpose of Socratic questions is to bring attention to relevant information that may be outside your focus and to use that information to re-evaluate your belief about that issue. Remember how Justin let go of his negative belief through a simple question that focused on what was hidden behind the dominant belief system he was living? That question was the spring board for a massive change in his life. When working with cognitive restructuring it is important to slow down the process of your thinking and to make it conscious. It helps to do this as a written exercise in the beginning so that you break out of automatic thinking patterns.

> **TRY THIS: Socratic Inquiry Questions**
>
> Is this thought always true? What is hidden?
>
> Does this thought help me move forward or make me feel stuck?
>
> What would be different I did not hold on to this thought?
>
> What new information or ideas are available when I do not hold on to this thought?
>
> How would I behave differently without this thought or belief?
>
> What would the impact of this different behaviour be on my life?

Complementary practices include exercise in self-compassion introduced in chapter three. Numerous ideas for these types of practices can be found in Kristin Neff's website www.self-compassion.org. Forgiveness practices are also useful here. Forgiveness for self and others can be powerful in releasing trapped energy. Remember that forgiveness is not about letting yourself or others of the hook from an accountability perspective. Forgiveness allows for releasing resentment that bleeds energy without adding any value.

> **TRY THIS: Hawaiian Forgiveness Exercise**
>
> For when you are asking for forgiveness. This can be done as a meditation rather than as a live practice with a person. Focusing on the person Say:
>
> - I'm Sorry
> - Please forgive me
> - Thank you
> - I love you
>
> Allow emotions to arise without judgment and repeat process until you experience a shift.
>
> When focusing on forgiving you can use different language. Depending on the person you are focusing on you may want to try:
>
> - We are all human
> - I forgive you
> - I wish you peace
> - I wish myself peace

Finally, the simplest way to release involves relaxing your body. Remember that in neuromuscular lock your body is experiencing constriction which supports and reinforces the constriction in your mind and beliefs. In addition to the basic relaxation and centering exercises discussed earlier, creating a psychological sense of safety can be very powerful. Russell Kolts suggests a simple exercise to help you identify and sense into your own experience of safety so that you can activate it whenever you need to release from a state of neuromuscular lock.

> **TRY THIS: Examining the Safeness Response**
>
> Remember a time when you felt safe and completely comfortable. Or imagine what it would feel like to feel completely at ease, content and safe.
>
> What emotions do you experience? What are your physical sensations?
>
> Consider your attention. What do you focus on? Was your focus broad or narrow?
>
> What were you thinking about? How did your thoughts relate to your emotional experience?
>
> What did you want to do? What behaviour did you engage in?

Extend

Extending is fundamentally about co-creating the life you desire. Notice that I said co-creating not creating. This is because we don't have omnipotent power regardless of how well we cultivate our focus. We create our lives in the context of the world, not in isolation. Additionally, despite all the emphasis on the law of attraction and similar philosophies, our choices do not always occur in circumstances of our own making. Success, therefore, requires building healthy relationships and working with others effectively. Let's explore some ways in which you can build effective relationships.

First, you must start with a recognition and belief that other people also have value, needs and the right to live well. In this way, you can create a desire to build relationships by understanding other people's perspectives. Steven Covey refers to one of the 7 habits of highly effective people as "seek first to understand then to be understood." Seek to understand by learning how to listen effectively. Be

> **TRY THIS: Reflective Listening**
>
> Pay attention to the other person not the thoughts in your own head or your environment.
>
> The goal is to understand (not to agree or disagree)
>
> Reflect back to the other the content, feelings and meaning that you saw and heard.
>
> If the person nods in the affirmative then you have earned the right to speak.

present when listening, ask questions, reflect back the ideas and feelings you heard so that you can demonstrate that you understood or be provided further information that will clarify the communication.

Finally, maintain a strong-back and an open-heart. Remember, confidence is not certainty. Confidence involves humility. Be willing to be clear about your perspective while remaining open to understanding others' perspectives.

This "habit" can also be expanded to a willingness to "give before you receive." Be willing to share your knowledge and networks for the greater good. Additionally, look for and identify the potential in others and offer them help when you can. Be curious and ask questions about others.

Finally, you can achieve high quality connections

TRY THIS: Three Connections Exercise

1. Center in you body by identifying a time you felt connected to yourself, others or nature. Notice how your body feels when you feel connected.

2. Call to mind your personal community of care. Think about who supports you and who inspires you. These can be living people that you know personally or that you respect from afar. They can be ancestors or animals or spirit guides. Sense them around you spatially. Feel support coming from them. Absorb that support and then also send it out to others.

3. Create a simple intention to connect with and be helpful to others even as you pursue your own goals wholeheartedly. Cultivate a win/win attitude.

by demonstrating integrity with your values. When you can demonstrate competence and vulnerability (demonstrating your humanity) others will more easily connect with you and respect you; you gain credibility. This creates influence (instead of power through dominance) that allows you to pursue your goals with the help of others.

Of course, it is essential to maintain healthy boundaries as you engage in and build your community. If you are having difficulty connecting you can also start by creating a felt sense of connection. Try this "three connections" exercise that I adapted from Stephen Gilligan's work.

As we build relationships we can concurrently develop and pursue our goals. Goals provide direction for life and it is important to consciously choose our direction. Research on goals setting is extensive as is the research that highlights how to effectively achieve one's goals. I summarize much of this in a simple "Full Brain Integration" exercise on page 137. Notice that it is important to have clear goals that are meaningful to you.

If you are struggling with identifying clear and meaningful goals find a quiet place and begin centering yourself. Once centered ask and answer the following three question quickly (about one minute per question. Question 1: What do I want to experience from life? Question 2: How do I want to grow? Question 3: How do I want to serve (or make a difference)?

Alternatively, once centered say the following, "my deepest desire is to____" and complete this with five words or less. Do this several times. After each occasion, notice how strongly you resonate with the identified goal. Gilligan and Dilts in their book *The Hero's Journey* explore a number of ways to identify meaningful goals.

Peter Levesque and I created another useful strategy to help people identify where they want to put their attention and resources. We have our clients identify what they are good at, what they enjoy, and what is needed at work or in the world (see Figure 3 Venn-diagram)[15]. The center, where all three areas overlap, is the sweet spot. The goal is to identify what you are good at, enjoy and brings value to the world so that you can focus your energy in that direction. Pay attention also to where you want to grow (areas you enjoy and are needed but you are not good at yet) and put energy there as well lest you stagnate. You may also consider how to add social value to your hobbies such that they may move into the sweet spot. Be careful of spending too much time in areas that you do not enjoy, even if you are good at them, because life will feel like a grind.

Figure 3

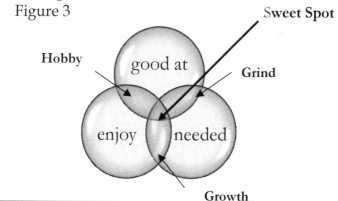

---

[15] Although we developed this independently, we later discovered a much older and more nuanced version that comes from the Japanese concept of Ikigai.

It is also important to share our goals so that they exist in the world of relationships and not just inside our own heads. There are many domains in life (work, family, friendships, health, etc.). Happiness research highlights that it is important to create meaningful goals across a variety of domains to lead a fulfilling life. For example, don't just focus on work success if your other life areas are suffering. You can choose two or three goals to work on from different domains at any one time.

You can see that the full brain integration exercise incorporates many of the practices discussed in this book. We center, we focus our attention on where we want to go and we open ourselves up to the steps we can take. Notice that the exercise finishes with taking action. Success in the end requires a willingness to be present and to invest energy into life affirming action so that you move towards your goals.

Finally, extending requires us to remember that life happens as we work on achieving these goals. Don't forget to live the journey. I'd like to conclude this section then by bringing you back to your values. To remembering that peace of mind comes from who you choose to be in the moments of your life, not merely in the achievement of your goals. Ground yourself in the person you wish to be. Cultivate your character, such that others know who you are, and you will find that others will be willing to help you achieve your goals. Try the "sort of person I want to be" exercise (page 138) regarding seeing your ideal self and then live that image. As Gandhi once said, "Be the change you wish to see in the world."

TRY THIS: Full Brain Integration

Write down your goal: (Be specific; it must be something you wish to create rather than something you wish to end).

Write down WHY you want to achieve this goal:

With whom did you/will you share this goal:

<u>Daily Exercise</u>

Step One: 1-2 minutes Centering (e.g., meditation or relaxation)

Step Two: Left Brain Focus

Identify 1 or 2 positive statements in the present tense regarding what you might say or hear as if you have already achieved the goal. Repeat these for 30 seconds

Step Three: Right Brain Focus

Identify an image of what you will see once you have achieved the goals. Fully engage in this image for 30 seconds as if it has already happened.

Step Four: Limbic System

Step into the felt sense of the emotion you will experience once you have achieved this goal. Feel it for 30 seconds

Step Five: Prefrontal Cortex

Return to the present by focusing on one thing you are currently grateful for in your life. Feel the gratitude somatically. Do this for one minute.

Step Six: Identify Action

From this state identify one gesture you can do today that will move you closer to your goal.

Step Seven: Take action identified in step six.

TRY THIS: The sort of person I want to be exercise

Take a moment to consider the sort of person you would like to be. Imagine some point in the future where you died and the people that love you most were at the funeral. Imagine the eulogy they would put together about how you lived your dash.

If you had lived your deepest values what words would you want them to say? Come up with three words that finish the sentence: S/He was so_____

_____

_____

_____

Now write a more detailed description of the type of person you'd like to be. What qualities would you like to have? How would you like others to feel when you are around? What feelings would you like your days to be filled with? What goals would you pursue?

_____
_____
_____
_____
_____
_____
_____
_____
_____
_____

Conclusion

As noted at the beginning of this chapter, there are many ways to work on your CORE. You can work with the exercises provided here or other ideas you have developed yourself or read about. Perhaps you will want to seek help from a therapist or a coach. As you engage in your life, keep these eight choices and four CORE principles in mind and I believe you will have a road map that will help you move more effectively through your life.

When you lose your footing, remember to center. When you lose perspective, practice opening. When you feel trapped by some idea or emotion, practice releasing. Finally, I invite you to extend into your life with a strong back and an open heart, with persistence and gentleness, with intelligent compassion. In doing so you will not avoid pain or errors but you will find beauty in the imperfect road ahead and within that imperfection you will experience success and contentment.

SOURCE NOTES

Introduction

Hadfield, C. (2013). *An astronaut's guide to life on Earth*. Toronto: Random House Canada.
Peat, D. (1997). *Infinite Potential: The Life and Times of David Bohm*. Reading, MA: Addison-Wesley

Chapter 1

Opening Quote: Yapko, M. (2011). *Mindfulness and Hypnosis*. New York: Norton
Achor, S. (2013). *Before Happiness: The 5 hidden keys to achieving success, spreading happiness and sustaining positive change*. NY: Random House.
Erskine, JA & Georgiou, GJ (2010), Effects of thought suppression on eating behaviour in restrained and non-restrained eaters. *Appetite*. 54(3): 499-503.
Kabat-Zinn, J. (1990). *Full catastrophe living: Using the wisdom of your body and mind to face stress, pain and illness*. New York, NY: Delacorte.
Kahneman, D (2011) *Thinking, Fast and Slow*. Toronto: Doubleday.
Keating, T. Centering Prayer instructions by Fr. Thomas Keating: https://cpt.org//files/WS%20-%20Centering%20Prayer.pdf
Seligman, M (1991). *Learned Optimism: How to Change your Mind and Your Life*. New York: Pocket Books.
Simons, D. J., & Chabris, C. F. (1999). Gorillas in our

midst: Sustained inattentional blindness for dynamic events. *Perception, 28*(9), 1059-1074.

Wegner DM, Schneider DJ, Carter SR, White TL. Paradoxical Effects of Thought Suppression. *Journal of Personality and Social Psychology,* 53, 5-13.

Wegner DM, Erber R. The Hyperaccessibility of Suppressed Thoughts. *Journal of Personality and Social Psychology*, 63, 903-912.

Wegner DM. Ironic Processes of Mental Control. *Psychological Review*, 101, 34-52.

Wegner DM, Gold DB. Fanning Old Flames - Emotional and Cognitive Effects of Suppressing Thoughts of a Past Relationship. *Journal of Personality and Social Psychology,* 68, 782-792.

Chapter 2

Opening quote by Thich Nhat Hanh (2007). For a Future to be Possible.: Buddhist Ethics for Everyday Life. Berkeley: Parallax Press.

Achor, S. (2013). *Before Happiness: The 5 hidden keys to achieving success, spreading happiness and sustaining positive change*. NY: Random House.

Atchley RA, Strayer DL, Atchley P (2012) Creativity in the Wild: Improving Creative Reasoning through Immersion in Natural Settings. *PLoS ONE* 7(12): e51474. http://doi.org/10.1371/journal.pone.0051474

Bateson, M. Nettle, D & Roberts, G. (2006). Cues of being watched enhance cooperation in real-world setting. *Biological Letters*, 2, 412-414.

Bargh, J. A., Chen, M., & Burrows, L. (1996). Automaticity of social behavior: Direct effects of trait construct and stereotype activation on action. *Journal of personality and social psychology, 71*(2), 230.

Cesario, J., Plaks, J., & Higgins, E. T. (2006). Automatic social behavior as motivated preparation to interact. *Journal of Personality and Social Psychology, 90,* 893-910.

DeCoster, J., & Claypool, H. M. (2004). A meta-analysis of priming effects on impression formation supporting a general model of informational biases. *Personality and Social Psychology Review,* 8, 2-27. doi: 10.1207/S15327957PSPR0801_1

Hogan (2011). *The Science of Influence.* John Wiley and Sons, New Jersey.

Kahneman, D. (2011). *Thinking, Fast and Slow.* Doubleday Canada

Hull, J., Slone, L., Metayer, K., & Matthews, A. (2002). The nonconsciousness of self-consciousness. *Journal of Personality and Social Psychology,* 83, 406-4254.

Kross, E., Verduyn, P., Demiralp, E., Park, J., & Lee, D. S. (2013). Facebook Use Predicts Declines in Subjective Well-Being in Young Adults. *PLoS ONE, 8*(8).

Lewis, S. J. & Harder, D. W. (1988). Velten's mood induction technique: "real" change and the effects of personality and sex on affect state. *Journal of Clinical Psychology.* 44. 441 - 444.

Mahowald, K., et al. A meta-analysis of syntactic priming in language production. *Journal of Memory and Language* (2016), http://dx.doi.org/10.1016/j.jml.2016.03.009

McGonigal, K. (2012). *The willpower instinct: How self-control works, why it matters, and what you can do to get more of it.* NY: Avery.

Shakya, H. B., & Christakis, N. A. (2017). Association of Facebook use with compromised well-being: a longitudinal study. *American journal of epidemiology, 185*(3), 203-211.

Velten, E. (1968). A laboratory task for induction of mood states. *Behavior Research and Therapy.* 6, 473 - 482.

Vohs, K., Mead, N. & Goode, M. (2006) The psychological consequences of money. *Science*, 314, 1154-1156.

Chapter 3

Opening quote: Osho (2009). *The Mustard Seed: The revolutionary Teachings of Jesus.* NY: OSHO Medial International

Carson, C (ed.) 1988. *The Autobiography of Martin Luther King Jr.* NY: Warner Books.

Frankl, Viktor E. (1962). *Man's search for meaning; an introduction to logotherapy.* Boston: Beacon Press.

Gilbert, P. (2009). *The compassionate mind.* London: Constable.

Also resources by Paul Gilbert on compassion: https://compassionatemind.co.uk/

Kornfield J. (2008). *The Art of Forgiveness, Lovingkindness and Peace.* NY: Bantam Books.

McGonigal, K. (2012). *The willpower instinct: How self-control works, why it matters, and what you can do to get more of it.* NY: Avery.

Neff, K. D. (2015). *Self-Compassion: The Proven Power of Being Kind to Yourself.* NY: Harper Collins

Neff, K. D. (2012). The science of self-compassion. In C. Germer & R. Siegel (Eds.), *Compassion and Wisdom in Psychotherapy* (pp. 79-92). New York: Guilford Press.

Neff Kristin: http://self-compassion.org/

Chapter 4

Opening quote: Isaacs, W. (2007). Einstein: His Life and Universe. NY: Simon & Schuster.

Alhola, P., & Polo-Kantola, P. (2007). Sleep deprivation: Impact on cognitive performance. *Neuropsychiatric disease and treatment*, 3(5), 553.

American Psychological Association and American Sleep Association recommendations on sleep hygiene: http://www.apa.org/helpcenter/sleep-disorders.aspx
https://www.sleepassociation.org/patients-general-public/insomnia/sleep-hygiene-tips/

Baldwin Jr, D. C., & Daugherty, S. R. (2004). Sleep deprivation and fatigue in residency training: results of a national survey of first-and second-year residents. *Sleep*, 27(2), 217-223.

Barton, J. & Pretty, J. (2010) What is the Best Dose of Nature and Green Exercise for Improving Mental Health? A Multi-Study Analysis. *Environmental Science & Technology*, 2010: 100325142930094 DOI: 10.1021/es903183r

Beaudoin, L. P., Hyniewska, S., & Bastien, C. (2017). Towards an affective information-processing theory of sleep onset and insomnia. Forthcoming (accepted) ISRE–2017 conference presentation. Abstract available from http://summit.sfu.ca/item/16915

Driver, H. S., & Taylor, S. R. (2000). Exercise and sleep. *Sleep medicine reviews*, 4(4), 387-402.

Deslandes, A., Moraes, H., Ferreira, C., Veiga, H., Silveira, H., Mouta, R., & Laks, J. (2009). Exercise and mental health: many reasons to move. *Neuropsychobiology, 59*(4), 191-198.

Denson, T. F., Capper, M. M., Oaten, M., Friese, M., & Schofield, T. P. (2011). Self-control training decreases aggression in response to provocation in aggressive individuals. *Journal of Research in Personality, 45*(2), 252-256.

Ganis, G., Thompson, W., Kosslyn, S (2004). Brain areas underlying visual mental imagery and visual perception: an fMRI study. *Cognitive Brain research*, 20, 226-241.

Gelbard-Sagiv H[1], Mukamel R, Harel M, Malach R, Fried I. (2008). Internally generated reactivation of single neurons in human hippocampus during free recall. *Science.* 3;322(5898):96-101. doi: 10.1126/science.1164685. Epub 2008 Sep 4.

Grant, A. (2014) Give and Take: A revolutionary approach to success. London: Weidenfield & Nicolson.

Harrison, Y., & Horne, J. A. (2000). The impact of sleep deprivation on decision making: a review. *Journal of experimental psychology: Applied, 6*(3), 236.

Jabr, F. (2013). Why your brain needs more downtime. *Scientific America.* www.scientificamerican.com/article/mental-downtime/

Ji, J. L., Heyes, S. B., MacLeod, C., & Holmes, E. A. (2016). Emotional mental imagery as simulation of reality: fear and beyond—a tribute to Peter Lang. *Behavior therapy, 47*(5), 702-719.

Lockley, S. W., Barger, L. K., Ayas, N. T., Rothschild, J. M., Czeisler, C. A., & Landrigan, C. P. (2007). Effects of health care provider work hours and sleep deprivation on safety and performance. *The Joint*

Commission Journal on Quality and Patient Safety, 33(11), 7-18.

Neal D. Wood, W, Wu, M Kurlander D. (2011) The Pull of the Past: When Do Habits Persist Despite Conflict With Motives? *Personality and Social Psychology Bulletin.* 37 (11), 1428-1437 DOI: https://doi.org/10.1177/0146167211419863

Norton, A. R., & Abbott, M. J. (2016). The efficacy of imagery rescripting compared to cognitive restructuring for social anxiety disorder. *Journal of anxiety disorders, 40,* 18-28.

Puets, TW, Flowers, S. & O'Connor, P.J. (2008) *Psychotherapy and Psychosomatics.* 77(3):167-74. doi: 10.1159/000116610. Epub 2008 Feb 14.

Reid, K. J., Baron, K. G., Lu, B., Naylor, E., Wolfe, L., & Zee, P. C. (2010). Aerobic exercise improves self-reported sleep and quality of life in older adults with insomnia. *Sleep medicine, 11*(9), 934-940.

Schwartz, A., Mori, M., Gao, R., NAIL, L., & KING, M. (2001). Exercise reduces daily fatigue in women with breast cancer receiving chemotherapy. *Medicine & Science in Sports & Exercise, 33*(5), 718-723.

Singh, N. A., Clements, K. M., & Fiatarone, M. A. (1997). A randomized controlled trial of the effect of exercise on sleep. *Sleep, 20*(2), 95-101.

Slimani, M., Tod, D., Chaabene, H., Miarka, B., & Chamari, K. (2016). Effects of Mental Imagery on Muscular Strength in Healthy and Patient Participants: A Systematic Review. *Journal of Sports Science & Medicine, 15*(3), 434–450.

Thompson, D. (2012). The case for vacation: Why science says breaks are good for productivity. *The Atlantic.*

https://www.theatlantic.com/business/archive/2012/08/the-case-for-vacation-why-science-says-breaks-are-good-for-productivity/260747/

Exercise:

Mayo Clinic exercise recommendations: http://www.mayoclinic.org/healthy-lifestyle/fitness/expert-answers/exercise/faq-20057916

Guidelines developed by the Canadian Society for Exercise Physiology (2011), www.activecanada2020.ca/active-canada-20-20/why-a-physical-activity-strategy-is-needed/physical-activity-sedentary-recommendations

University of Georgia. (2006, November 8). Regular Exercise Plays A Consistent And Significant Role In Reducing Fatigue. *ScienceDaily*. Retrieved August 5, 2017 from www.sciencedaily.com/releases/2006/11/061101151005.htm

Award winning commercial by Snickers playing off the "Hangry" experience. http://ww.adweek.com/brand-marketing/snickers-brady-bunch-ad-wins-first-sup

Domestic violence resources:

http://www.justice.gc.ca/eng/cj-jp/fv-vf/help-aide.html
http://endingviolencecanada.org/
http://ncadv.org/learn-more/resources
http://www.thehotline.org/

Chapter 5

Aspin, L & Tedeschi, R. (2010). The value of positive psychology for health psychology: Progress and pitfalls in examining the relation of positive phenomenon to health. *American Behavioral Medicine*, 39, 4-15.

Baker, J., Kelly, C., Calhoun, G., Cann, A & Tedeschi, R. (2008). An examination of posttramatic growth and posttraumatic depreciation: Two exploratory studies. *Journal of Loss and Trauma*, 13, 450-465.

Bennet-Goleman, T *Emotional Alchemy: How the Mind can Heal the Heart*. NY: Harmony.

Calhoun, L & Tedeschi, R. (2004). The foundations of posttraumatic growth: New consideration. *Psychological Inquiry*, 15, 93-102.

Coelho Paulo (1993). *The Alchemist*. NY: Harper Collins

Erikson, M. - The seminars, workshops and lectures of Milton H. Erickson, volume II: life reframing in hypnosis. *Edited by Ernest L. Rossi and Margaret O. Ryan. Free Association Books, London. 1998.*

Fredrikson B. (2009) *Positivity: Top Notch research reveals the 3 to 1 ratio that will change your life*. NY: Random House

Yapko, M. (2003). *Trancework: An introduction to the practice of clinical hypnosis*. New York: Routledge.

Watzlawwick, P, Weakland, J. & Fisch, R. (1974). Change. NY: Norton.

Terry Waite story: http://www.telegraph.co.uk/men/thinking-man/terry-waite-i-spent-five-years-as-a-hostage-in-beirut---but-i-ne/

Chapter 6

Opening Quote: Tom Robbins from NY Times article by Thomas Egan. IN THE CREATIVE PROCESS WITH: Tom Robbins; Perfect Sentences, Imperfect Universe: http://www.nytimes.com/1993/12/30/garden/in-the-creative-process-with-tom-robbins-perfect-sentences-imperfect-universe.html?pagewanted=all

Beecher, H. K (1955). The power of Placebo. *JAMA* 159, 1602-1606

Crum, A., Salavoy, P. Achor, S. (2013). Rethinking stress: The role of mindsets in determining stress response. *Journal of Personality and Social Psychology*, 2013, Vol. 104, No. 4, 716–733

Dweck, C. (2007). Mindset: *The new psychology of success*. NY: Ballantine Books.

Dr. Carol Dweck ted talk: www.ted.com/talks/carol_dweck_the_power_of_believing_that_you_can_improve

Lipton, B. (2005). *The Biology of Belief*. Santa Rosa CA: Elite Books.

Kelly McGonigal referred to the study regarding stress and belief in her Ted talk: https://www.ted.com/talks/kelly_mcgonigal_how_to_make_stress_your_friend

Pulos, L (1990). *Beyond Hypnosis*. San Francisco: Omega Press.

Putting Placebo to Work. *Harvard Health Letter* {http://www.health.harvard.edu/newsletters/harvard_health_letter/2012/april}

Spectre, M. The power of nothing. *Annals of Science*. December 12, 2011 Issue.

Wampold, B, Imel, Z & Minami, T. (2007). The Placebo Effect: "Relatively Large" and "Robust" Enough to Survive Another Assault. *Journal of Clinical Psychology*, Vol. 63(4), 401–403

Chapter 7

Opening quote: Ursula K Le Guin (1969). *The Left Hand of Darkness*. New York: Ace Science Fiction Books

Armstrong, K. (2009). *The Case for God*. NY: Random House.

Berridge, K. C., & Robinson, T. E. (1998). What is the role of dopamine in reward: hedonic impact, reward learning, or incentive salience?. *Brain research reviews*, *28*(3), 309-369.

Covey, S. R. (1997). *The 7 habits of highly effective families: Building a beautiful family culture in a turbulent world*. New York: Golden Books.

Dahlsgaard, K., Peterson, C., & Seligman, M. E. (2005). Shared virtue: The convergence of valued human strengths across culture and history. *Review of general psychology*, *9*(3), 203.

Flagel, S. B., Clark, J. J., Robinson, T. E., Mayo, L., Czuj, A., Willuhn, I., & Akil, H. (2011). A selective role for dopamine in reward learning. *Nature*, *469*(7328), 53.

Grant, A. (2014) *Give and Take: A revolutionary approach to success*. London: Weidenfield & Nicolson.

Peterson, C., & Seligman, M. E. (2004). *Character strengths and virtues: A handbook and classification* (Vol. 1). Oxford University Press.

Saridid, G (ed). 1992. *C.P. Cavafy Collected Poems*. Princeton: Princeton University Press.

Seligman, M. E., & Csikszentmihalyi, M. (2014).

Positive psychology: An introduction. In *Flow and the foundations of positive psychology* (pp. 279-298). Springer Netherlands.

Grant, A. (2014) *Give and Take: A revolutionary approach to success.* London: Weidenfield & Nicolson.

Michell Watt media stories:
http://www.abc.net.au/news/2012-08-05/scathing-watt-tells-media-to-27wake-up27/4178492

https://www.pedestrian.tv/sport/olympic-medalist-mitchell-watt-tells-australian-media-to-wake-up/

Safra Catz new story in business insider: http://www.businessinsider.com/oracle-ceo-safra-catz-on-sap-2015-5

Chapter 8

Opening quote: Rev Henry Melville: The Golden lectures, sermons delivered at St. Margaret's church, Lothbury, 1853 (-56). Selected from the Penny pulpit

Ahuvia, A., Thin, N., Haybron, D. M., Biswas-Diener, R., Ricard, M., & Timsit, J. (2015). Happiness: An interactionist perspective. *International Journal of Wellbeing, 5*(1), 1-18. doi:10.5502/ijw.v5i1.1

Aknin, L. B., Barrington-Leigh, C. P., Dunn, E. W., Helliwell, J. F., Burns, J., Biswas-Diener, R., . . . Norton, M. I. (2013). Prosocial spending and well-being: Cross-cultural evidence for a psychological universal. *Journal of Personality and Social Psychology, 104*(4), 635-652. http://dx.doi.org/10.1037/a0031578

Ashar, Y. K., Andrews-Hanna, J. R., Dimidjian, S.,

& Wager, T. D. (2016). *Towards a Neuroscience of Compassion: A Brain-Systems-Based Model and Research Agenda. Positive Neuroscience Handbook.*

Barraza, J. A., & Zak, P. J. (2009). Empathy toward strangers triggers oxytocin release and subsequent generosity. *Annals of the New York Academy of Sciences, 1167*(1), 182-189.

Childre, D. (2010). Coherence: bridging personal, social, and global health. *Alternative Therapies in Health and Medicine, 16*(4), 10.

Coffey, K. A., Hartman, M., & Fredrickson, B. L. (2010). Deconstructing mindfulness and constructing mental health: understanding mindfulness and its mechanisms of action. *Mindfulness, 1*(4), 235-253.

Csaszar, I., & Curry, J. R. (2010). Loving kindness meditation: A promising practice for reducing stress and increasing empathy. *VISTAS Online, 86*, 1-11.

Dunn, E. W., Aknin, L. B., & Norton, M. I. (2008). Spending money on others promotes happiness. *Science, 319*(5870), 1687-1688.

Fosha, D., Siegel, D. J., & Solomon, M. (Eds.). (2009). *The healing power of emotion: Affective neuroscience, development & clinical practice.* WW Norton & Company.

Fredrickson, Barbara L. "Positive emotions broaden and build." *Advances in experimental social psychology* 47.1 (2013): 53.

Fredrickson, B. L. (2004). The broaden-and-build theory of positive emotions. *Philosophical Transactions of the Royal Society B: Biological Sciences, 359*(1449), 1367.

Gilbert, P and Procter, S (2006) Compassionate Mind Training for People with High Shame and Self-Criticism: Overview and Pilot Study of a Group

Therapy Approach, *Clinical Psychology and Psychotherapy*, 13, 353-379

Gilligan, S. (2012). *Generative Trance: The Experience of Creative Flow*. Crown House Publishing

Goleman, D., & Boyatzis, R. (2008). Social intelligence and the biology of leadership. *Harvard Business Review, 86*(9), 74-81.

Iacoboni, M. (2009). Imitation, empathy, and mirror neurons. *Annual review of psychology, 60*, 653-670.

Johnson, D. P., Penn, D. L., Fredrickson, B. L., Meyer, P. S., Kring, A. M., & Brantley, M. (2009). Loving-kindness meditation to enhance recovery from negative symptoms of schizophrenia. *Journal of clinical psychology, 65*(5), 499-509.

Junger, S (2016). *Tribe: On Homecoming and Belonging*. Toronto: Harper Collins.

Kok, B. E., & Fredrickson, B. L. (2010). Upward spirals of the heart: Autonomic flexibility, as indexed by vagal tone, reciprocally and prospectively predicts positive emotions and social connectedness. *Biological psychology, 85*(3), 432-436.

Kok, B. E., Coffey, K. A., Cohn, M. A., Catalino, L. I., Vacharkulksemsuk, T., Algoe, S. B., ... & Fredrickson, B. L. (2013). How positive emotions build physical health: Perceived positive social connections account for the upward spiral between positive emotions and vagal tone. *Psychological science, 24*(7), 1123-1132.

Lambert, M. J., & Barley, D. E. (2001). Research summary on the therapeutic relationship and psychotherapy outcome. *Psychotherapy: Theory, research, practice, training, 38*(4), 357.

Lutz, A., Brefczynski-Lewis, J., Johnstone, T., & Davidson, R. J. (2008). Regulation of the neural circuitry of emotion by compassion meditation: effects of meditative expertise. *PloS one, 3*(3), e1897.

Leary, M. R., Tate, E. B., Adams, C. E., Batts Allen, A., & Hancock, J. (2007). Self-compassion and reactions to unpleasant self-relevant events: the implications of treating oneself kindly. *Journal of personality and social psychology, 92*(5), 887.

Martin, D. J., Garske, J. P., & Davis, M. K. (2000). Relation of the therapeutic alliance with outcome and other variables: a meta-analytic review.

McCraty, R., & Zayas, M. A. (2014). Cardiac coherence, self-regulation, autonomic stability, and psychosocial well-being. *Frontiers in psychology, 5*.

Mikolajczak, M., Gross, J. J., Lane, A., Corneille, O., de Timary, P., & Luminet, O. (2010). Oxytocin makes people trusting, not gullible. *Psychological Science, 21*(8), 1072-1074.

Morley, C. A., & Kohrt, B. A. (2013). Impact of peer support on PTSD, hope, and functional impairment: a mixed-methods study of child soldiers in Nepal. *Journal of Aggression, Maltreatment & Trauma, 22*(7), 714-734.

Nakagawa, Y., & Shaw, R. (2004). Social capital: A missing link to disaster recovery. *International Journal of Mass Emergencies and Disasters, 22*(1), 5-34.

Neff, K. D. (2012). The science of self-compassion. In C. Germer & R. Siegel (Eds.), *Compassion and Wisdom in Psychotherapy* (pp. 79-92). New York: Guilford Press.

Norris, F. H., Stevens, S. P., Pfefferbaum, B., Wyche, K. F., & Pfefferbaum, R. L. (2008). Community resilience as a metaphor, theory, set of capacities, and strategy for disaster readiness. *American journal of community psychology, 41*(1-2), 127-150.

Porges, S. W. (2007). The polyvagal perspective. *Biological psychology, 74*(2), 116-143.

Porges, S. W. (2007). The Polyvagal Perspective. *Biological Psychology, 74*(2), 116-143. http://doi.org/10.1016/j.biopsycho.2006.06.009

Porges, S. W. (2009). Reciprocal influences between body and brain in the perception and expression of affect. *The Healing Power of Emotions: Affective Neuroscience, Development, and Clinical Practice*, 27-54.

Schwartz, J. M., & Begley, S. (2009). *The mind and the brain*. Springer Science & Business Media.

Seppela, A. (2012). How the stress of disasters brings people together. Scientific America. November 6, 2012. https://www.scientificamerican.com/article/how-the-stress-of-disaster-brings-people-together/

Seligman, M. (2002). *Authentic Happiness*. Free press: New York.

Siegel, D. J. (2007). *The mindful brain: Reflection and attunement in the cultivation of well-being*. WW Norton & Company.

Solomon, R. L. (1980). The opponent-process theory of acquired motivation: The costs of pleasure and the benefits of pain. *American psychologist, 35*(8), 691.

Staub, E. (2004). Basic human needs, altruism, and aggression. *The social psychology of good and evil*, 51-84.

Stefanakis, H. (2008). Caring and compassion when working with offenders of crime and violence. *Violence and victims, 23*(5), 652-661.

von Dawans B., Fischbacher U., Kirschbaum C., Fehr E., and Heinrichs M. (2012). The social dimension of stress reactivity: acute stress increases prosocial behavior in humans. *Psychological Science*, 23, 651-660.

Weng, H. Y., Fox, A. S., Shackman, A. J., Stodola, D.

E., Caldwell, J. Z., Olson, M. C., ... & Davidson, R. J. (2013). Compassion training alters altruism and neural responses to suffering. *Psychological science, 24*(7), 1171-1180.

WHO 2017- World Happiness Report http://worldhappiness.report/ed/2017/

Zak, P. J., Stanton, A. A., & Ahmadi, S. (2007). Oxytocin increases generosity in humans. *PloS one, 2*(11), e1128.

Chapter 9

Achor, S. (2013). *Before Happiness: The 5 hidden keys to achieving success, spreading happiness and sustaining positive change.* NY: Random House.

Berger, W. (2014). *A More Beautiful Question.* NY: Bloomsbury.

Brown, R., Chevalier, G., & Hill, M. (2015). Grounding after moderate eccentric contractions reduces muscle damage. *Open access journal of sports medicine, 6,* 305.

Chevalier, G. (2015). The effect of grounding the human body on mood. *Psychological reports, 116*(2), 534-542.

Childre, D., & Rozman, D. (2005). *Transforming stress: The HeartMath solution for relieving worry, fatigue, and tension.* New Harbinger Publications.

Coffey, K. A., Hartman, M., & Fredrickson, B. L. (2010). Deconstructing mindfulness and constructing mental health: understanding mindfulness and its mechanisms of action. *Mindfulness, 1*(4), 235-253.

Covey, S. R. (1997). *The 7 habits of highly effective families: Building a beautiful family culture in a turbulent world*. New York: Golden Books.

De Mello, A. (1990). *Awareness: The Perils and Opportunities of Reality*. NY: Doubleday.

Gilligan, S. (2012). *Generative trance: The experience of creative flow*. Crown House Publishing.

Gilligan, S. & Dilts, R (2009). *The Hero's Journey*. Bethel CT: Crown Publishing.

Goldin, P. R., McRae, K., Ramel, W., & Gross, J. J. (2008). The neural bases of emotion regulation: reappraisal and suppression of negative emotion. *Biological psychiatry, 63*(6), 577-586.

Grant, A. (2014) *Give and Take: A revolutionary approach to success*. London: Weidenfield & Nicolson.

Ikigai image see: https://upload.wikimedia.org/wikipedia/commons/1/18/Ikigai-EN.svg

James, M. (2011). The Hawaiian Secret of Forgiveness. *Psychology Today*. www.psychologytoday.com/blog/focus-forgiveness/201105/the-hawaiian-secret-forgiveness

Jazaieri, H., Jinpa, G. T., McGonigal, K., Rosenberg, E. L., Finkelstein, J., Simon-Thomas, E., ... & Goldin, P. R. (2013). Enhancing compassion: a randomized controlled trial of a compassion cultivation training program. *Journal of Happiness Studies, 14*(4), 1113-1126.

Kolts, R (2012). *The Compassionate Mind Guide to Managing Anger*. Oakland: New Harbinger Publications.

Kornfield, J. (2002). *The Art of Forgiveness, Lovingkindness and Peace*. NY: Bantam.

Kuyken, W., Weare, K., Ukoumunne, O., Vicary, R., Motton, N., Burnett, R., Cullen, C., Hennelly, S., & Huppert, F. (2013). Effectiveness of the Mindfulness in Schools Program: Non-randomized controlled feasibility study. *The British Journal of Psychiatry 203(2)*, 1-6.

Lehrer, P. M., & Gevirtz, R. (2014). Heart rate variability biofeedback: how and why does it work? *Frontiers in psychology, 5.*

Lutz, A., Dunne, J. D., & Davidson, R. J. (2007). Meditation and the neuroscience of consciousness. *Cambridge handbook of consciousness*, 499-555.

McCraty, R., & Zayas, M. A. (2014). Cardiac coherence, self-regulation, autonomic stability, and psychosocial well-being. *Frontiers in psychology, 5.*

Oschman, J. L., Chevalier, G., & Brown, R. (2015). The effects of grounding (earthing) on inflammation, the immune response, wound healing, and prevention and treatment of chronic inflammatory and autoimmune diseases. *Journal of inflammation research, 8,* 83.

Padesky, C. A. (1993, September). Socratic questioning: Changing minds or guiding discovery. In *A keynote address delivered at the European Congress of Behavioural and Cognitive Therapies, London* (Vol. 24). padesky.com/newpad/wp-content/uploads/2012/11/socquest.pdf

Peterson C (2008) Ikigai and mortality, *Psychology Today,* https://www.psychologytoday.com/blog/the-good-life/200809/ikigai-and-mortality

Siegel, D. J. (2001). Toward an interpersonal neurobiology of the developing mind: Attachment relationships, "mindsight," and neural integration. *Infant mental health journal, 22*(1-2), 67-94.

Song, H. S., & Lehrer, P. M. (2003). The effects of specific respiratory rates on heart rate and heart rate variability. *Applied psychophysiology and biofeedback, 28*(1), 13-23.

Quoidbach, J., Mikolajczak, M., & Gross, J. J. (2015). Positive interventions: An emotion regulation perspective. *Psychological Bulletin, 141*(3), 655.

Images

Book Cover image: Nature Path by Wendy McKinlay. www.mckinlayphoto.com Original photo. Used with permission of the artist.

Steering wheel image: photo by Warwick Carter adapted to pencil drawing is licensed under CC BY-NC https://www.flickr.com/photos/warwick_carter/5328324421/

Skid Mark image: Photo by j-ster is licensed under CC BY-NC-SA 2.0 source: jennettefulda.com /wp-content/uploads/2014/06/skid-marks.jpg

Tree Man image: by Wendy McKinlay. Original photo. Used with permission of the artist.

Brain Gears image: chrome://global/skin/media imagedoc-darknoise.png is licensed under CC BY

Climbing out image: drawing by the author.

Bicycle image: https://openclipart.org/detail/12905/bike by maxib's Clipart

Lemonade: https://openclipart.org/image/2400px

/svg_to_png/252280/Cold-Glass-Of-Lemonade.png

Trickster: https://commons.wikimedia.org/wiki/File:_Trickster_-_Print_by_Bill_Lewis.jpg is licensed under CC BY-SA

Nature Path: by Wendy McKinlay. Original photo changed to pencil drawing by the author. Used with permission of the artist.

Community/Connection: by Unknown Author is licensed under CC BY-SA source: https://fabiusmaximus.files.wordpress.com/2012/12/20121231-community-ring.jpg

Heart: Passion and Compassion by Gwen Mehrag source: http://www.drawneartogod.com/paintings/shared-heart-passion-and-compassion-prophetic-art-painting.jpg is licensed under CC BY-NC

Lion and Lamb: This Photo by Unknown Author is licensed under CC BY-NC-ND source: http://4.bp.blogspot.com/-TJUcksmOPJw/TZDWmOLBo4I/AAAAAAAAB8k/gWiEetgY66c/s1600/lion-and-the-lamb.jpg

Demonstrating compassion and care: Photo by Unknown Author is licensed under CC BY-NC source https://i1.wp.com/transitionofthoughts.com/wp-content/uploads/2015/02/o-compassion-facebook.jpg?resize=1024%2C51

ABOUT THE AUTHOR

Dr. Harry Stefanakis is clinical and consulting psychologist in private practice in Vancouver, British Columbia. He has over 20 years of experience facilitating individual and social change with an emphasis on intelligent compassion processes. As an internationally recognized educator and consultant, he has been a visiting expert for the United Nations: Asia and Far East Institute and provided training and consultation for various agencies and programs in Canada, the United States and Europe. He has participated in numerous initiatives on ending violence including the Be More Than A Bystander campaign. He is on the executive board of the Institute for Knowledge Mobilization and the board and faculty of the Canadian Society of Clinical Hypnosis (BC division). He can be found in the world wide web at: www.drharry.ca

Made in the USA
Columbia, SC
20 September 2017